RESTAURANT
SERVICE

MW00573660

PREPARATION
CARVING & SLICING
FLAMBÉING
SETTING THE TABLES
SERVICE

Thierry Boulicot
Dominique Jeuffrault

The photographs were taken at the Lycée Hôtelier de Blois (41000) and Grand Hôtel du Lion d'Or in Romorantin-Lanthenay (41200).

The authors would like to thank all of the establishments which lent their equipment and premises.

They would also like to greatly thank all of the colleagues and experts who helped them with this project.

Authors
Thierry Boulicot
Dominique Jeuffrault

Photographs
J.F Doré (Meilleur ouvrier de France)

Photographs
Stockfood/Sweet savoury: pp. 12, 20, 26, 90, 100, 198, 228, 232
Adobe stock: cutlery, pp.8, 14, 30, 50, 62, 64, 110, 118, 140, 160, 180, 182, 184, 187, 189, 192, 194, 212

Graphic design
Sandra Cantaloube
Adrien Midzic
Typefaces
Gotham, Bota

ISBN
9782857087687

Rights to all translation, adaptation and reproduction by any means reserved for all countries.

"Any representation or reproduction, in full or in part, of the texts and illustrations made without the consent of the author or their beneficiaries or concessionaires is illicit (French Law No. 57-298 of 11 March 1957, Article 40 paragraph 1). A representation or reproduction by any means whatsoever (photocopies, photos, films) shall constitute a punishable infringement under Article 425 and following the French Penal Code. Under paragraphs 2 and 3 of Article 41 of Law No. 52-298 of 11 March 1957 only copies or reproductions strictly for personal use and not any collective use, and analyses and short citations used solely for examples and illustrations are permitted."

Editions BPI
1 Boulevard des Bouvets
92 000 Nanterre

www.editions-bpi.fr
bpi@editions-bpi.fr

Only one method was retained for each item.

The technique recommended covers three fundamental aspects for beginners:

SIMPLE GESTURES
QUICK EXECUTION
CLASSICAL STYLE

There are, of course, other methods used in the industry than those selected.

ADDITIONAL COMMENTS

All of the items were prepared on a guéridon in front of a neatly served table to ensure proper organisation and cleanliness. However, some preparations - either because they take too long or are not visually of interest to the client - are sometimes carried out in the pantry. Such is the case for the following items:

Artichoke with vinaigrette page 66
Avocado and prawns page 68
Cocktail prawns page 72
Melon half page 80
Melon slices page 82
Cocktail grapefruit page 86
Flat and cupped oysters & muscles page 106
Beurre Suzette page 202
Pineapple page 214

Some preparations are also carried out at the buffet, including the following:

Foie gras page 76
cured ham page 92
York ham page 94
Pickled beef tongue, salami, dried sausage, Andouille de guéméné, pâté en croûte, terrine page 96
Smoked salmon page 112
Smoked eel and trout page 115
Cold salmon page 126

The **foie gras** (page 76) and **cold salmon** (page 126) may also be brought to the client.

Lastly, the different accompaniments and garnishes for the dishes were not included on the guéridon in order to focus solely on the preparation itself.

BPI CAMPUS
BEST PRACTICE INSIDE

1ST VIRTUAL CAMPUS FOR HOSPITALITY AND CULINARY ARTS INDUSTRY

1,000

VIDEOS TO UNDERSTAND AND EXECUTE TECHNICAL GESTURES

> *EXPERIMENTAL WORKSHOPS TO TRAIN STUDENTS BY ACCELERATING AND REINFORCING KNOWLEDGE ACQUISITION FOR GREATER SUCCESS*

300

TECHNICAL SHEETS TO PERFECT THE TECHNICAL KNOWLEDGE REQUIRED THROUGHOUT ONE'S PROFESSIONAL LIFE

> *QUIZZES TO INDEPENDENTLY EVALUATE YOUR KNOWLEDGE AND SKILLS*

WWW.BPI-CAMPUS.COM

OUR REFERENCE BOOKS

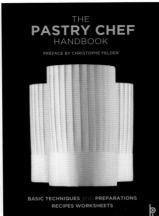

Already available in French

Digital version included

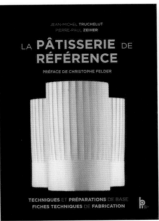

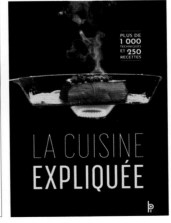

Editions BPI 2018—ISBN: 978-2-85708-768-7
All rights of translation, adaptation, and reproduction by any process are reserved for all countries.
"Any representation or reproduction, in whole or in part, of the texts and illustrations made without the consent of the authors or of their assignees or beneficiaries is unlawful (French Copyright law of March 11, 1957, paragraph 1 of Article 40). Such representation or reproduction, by any means whatsoever (photocopies, photos, films), constitutes an infringement that is punishable by Article 425 and following of the French Penal Code. The French Copyright law, under the provisions of paragraphs 2 and 3 of Article 41, authorizes only copies or reproductions strictly reserved for the copyist's personal use and not intended for collective use, and only analyzes and short quotations for the purpose of examples and information."

SUMMARY

CUTLERY & VARIOUS ACCESSORIES

CUTLERY

	NAME	FEATURES	USE
1	Hollow blade carving knife	30cm blade, flexible	Smoked salmon Ham on the bone
2	Carving knife	30cm blade, rigid	Leg cuts
3	Slicing knife	22 cm blade, rigid	Beef ribs Rack of veal
4	Serrated knife	19 cm blade, rigid and serrated	Pineapple
5	Sole knife	17 cm blade, flexible	Duck
6	Table knife	14 cm blade, rigid	Rack of lamb Chicken
7	Boning knife	11 cm blade, rigid	Ham on the bone
8	Paring knife	9 cm blade, rigid	Fruit

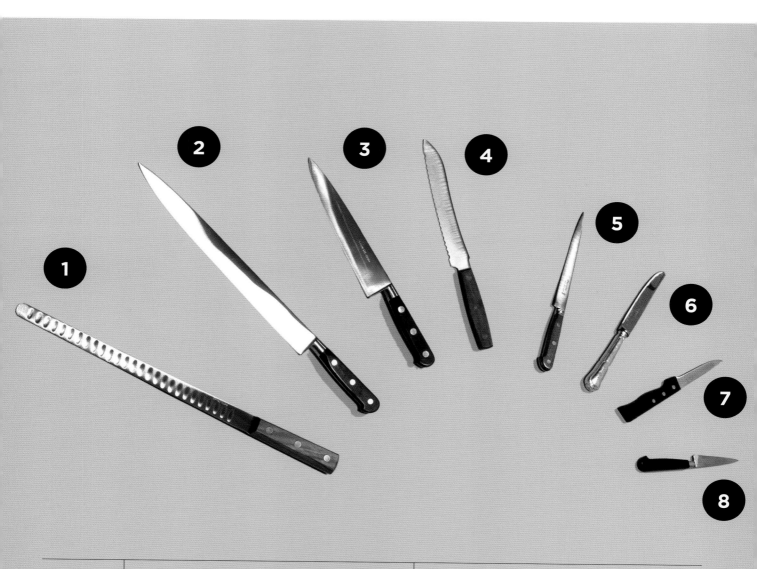

VARIOUS ACCESSORIES

	NAME	FEATURES	USE
9	Melon baller	25mm diameter	Melon
10	Lobster pick		Lobster/Spiny lobster
11	Oyster knife	Knife without a guard 6.5cm blade	Oysters
12	Salmon pliers		Smoked salmon
13	Nutcracker		Lobster
14	Whisk	70mm balloon diameter	Beurre Suzette

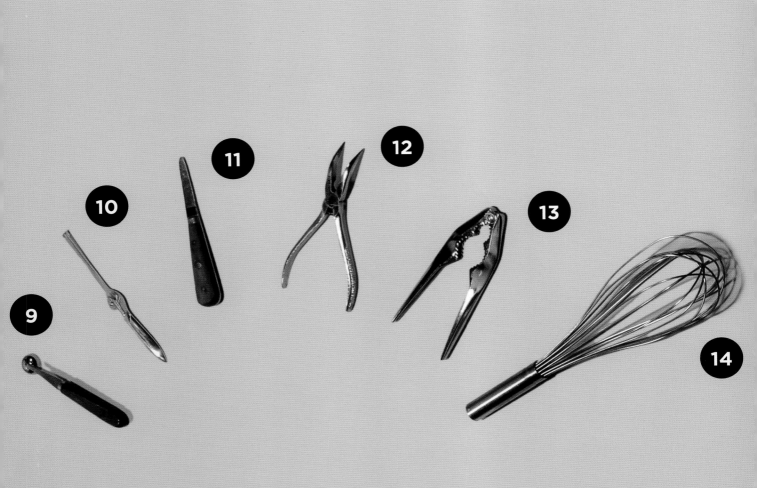

SETTING THE TABLES

13

RESTAURANT SERVICE

SETTING THE TABLES

13

SETTING THE TABLES

Restaurant ready for clients.

LINING

Table covered in a thick material (cotton) to prevent the tablecloths from getting worn too quickly and muffle noise.

Round table lined with 5 seats.
The chairs are placed around the table as described in the last example.

Round table lined with 5 seats.
Place a chair against one of the table legs to then place the other four chairs in the gaps.

Table with 6 seatss.
This table can be made up of one square table with 2 seats and one rectangular table with 4 seats.

Table with 8 seats.

Same table set up (square table and rectangular table).

Add two end seats.

SETTING UP DIFFERENT TABLE SHAPES

Square table with 2 seats.

Clients face to face.

Decorated with a vase and flowers.

Square table with 2 seats.

Clients side by side.

Decorated with a vase and flowers.

Table with 6 seats.

Square and rectangular table.

Tall floral decoration at the head of the table.

Table with 8 seats.

Square and rectangular table.

3 seats on each side and 2 end seats.

Low floral decoration.

Round table with 5 seats.

Low floral decoration in the centre.

PLACING THE TABLECLOTH

Placing the tablecloth on a rectangular table: stand at the long side of the table.

Placing the tablecloth on a square table: stand at one of the table sides.

Placing the tablecloth on a round table: stand between the table legs.

Unfold the tablecloth along its length (fold towards you).

Hold the final fold of the tablecloth between your fingers.

Free the last fold by lifting the other two.

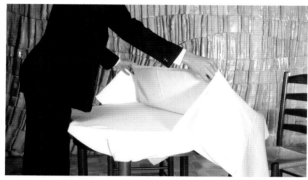

In a straight motion, place the tablecloth on the outside of the table while holding the upper folds.

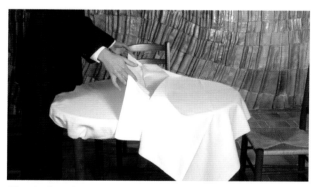

Check that the tablecloth is centred correctly and placed in the middle of the table.

Pull the middle fold after having gently freed the double fold.

Finish placing the tablecloth.

Check that the tablecloth is correctly aligned.

Once you are sure that the tablecloth is centred correctly and that the tablecloth corners are aligned with the table legs, place the chairs around the table.

A cloth may be placed on top of the tablecloth to protect it for longer.

The method used for the tablecloth should be applied for placing the cloth.

"À LA CARTE" SET-UP

Round table with 4 seats

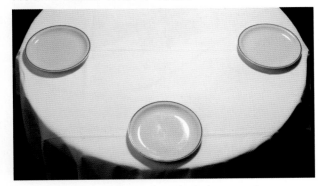

Place the plates in front of each chair, around a centimetre away from the table edge.

Place a large knife to the right of the plate edge, with the butt of the knife around a centimetre away from the table edge and the blade edge facing inwards.

Place a large fork in the same position to the left of the plate (prongs facing upwards).

Place a bread plate to the left of the large plate, level with the prongs of the large fork.

Place a dessert knife (butter knife) on the bread plate with the edge of the blade facing outwards.

Place a water glass above the centre of the plate.

Place a wine glass to the right of the water glass.

Note: turn the glasses over just before service.

Place the smaller pieces of tableware (salt & pepper shakers, water jug saucer, table number) in the centre of the table so that they can be accessed by all of the clients.

An ash tray may also be added.

Finish setting the table with a low (so as not to get in the way of the clients) floral decoration in the centre of the table, moving the smaller tableware out of the way.

Full view of tables set up for a banquet (round and oval tables) for a meal with entertainment.

"FIXED MENU" OR "BANQUET" SET-UP

Rectangular banquet table with 12 seats in a restaurant.

Oval skirted table:
Same set-up as for the round table.

Round skirted table:

Set-up:

Meat - Vegetables

- large knife,
- large fork.

Fish

- fish knife,
- fish fork.

Soups

- large spoon.

Cheese (in front of the plate)

- dessert knife,
- dessert fork.

Glasses

- water glass
- wine glass (one or two depending on the different wines to be served).

Small tableware (salt & pepper shakers, water jug saucer, table number, ash tray).

Low floral decoration in the centre.

Salad and dessert cutlery are placed on a separate service plate in advance to avoid overcrowding the table.

"Fixed menu" set-up

Meat – Vegetables

- large knife,
- large fork.

Fish

- fish knife,
- fish fork.

Starters

- dessert knife,
- dessert fork.

Salads (in front of the plate)

- dessert knife,
- dessert fork.

Ice cream

- dessert spoon.

Glasses

- water glass,
- white wine glass,
- red wine glass.

"GOURMET" SET-UP

Full view of a "gourmet" restaurant set-up.

"Gourmet" set-up:

- large base plate,
- bread plate,
- dessert knife (butter knife),
- water glass,
- napkin,
- small tableware (salt & pepper shakers, water jug saucer, table number),
- floral decoration,
- candle holder

With this set-up, the tableware can be laid out when the order is made based on the food and drinks ordered to avoid unnecessary interventions.

CARRYING TABLEWARE & CLEARING TABLES

CARRYING TABLEWARE & CLEARING TABLES

Carrying one plate. Careful! Do not put your thumb on the inner plate.

CARRYING PLATES

1st method

Carrying two plates with one hand.
Take the first plate in your left hand.
Leave your thumb and little finger free.

Place the second plate on your thumb, little finger and wrist protected by a cloth.
Check the plates are well balanced.

Carrying two plates with one hand.

Take the first plate in your left hand, with your thumb on the edge of the plate, known as "marli" or "marly".

Leave your little and ring finger completely free.

2nd method

Place the second plate under the first, holding it with your index, middle, ring and little finger.

Check the plates are well balanced.

3rd method

Place the second plate on your thumb, ring finger, little finger and wrist protected by a cloth.

Check the plates are well balanced.

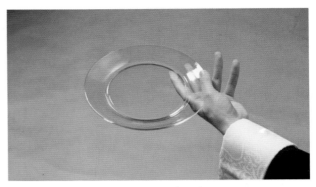

Carrying three plates with one hand.

Take the first plate in your left hand, with your thumb on the edge of the plate.

Leave your little and ring fingers completely free.

Place the second plate under the first, holding it with your index, middle and little finger.

Leave your little finger free.

Place the third plate on your thumb and little finger, with your wrist protected by a cloth.

Check the plates are well balanced.

CLEARING TABLES

Clear the first plate with your left hand, holding the large fork with your thumb (large knife crossed underneath).

Leave your ring and little finger free.

Place the second plate with the cutlery on your thumb, little finger and ring finger, with your wrist protected by a cloth.

Check the plates are well balanced.

Place the cutlery down on the lower plate, crossing them over to leave space for any waste.

Clear the third plate with the cutlery and place it on the top plate.

Continue clearing the table applying the method above.

CLEARING SOUP PLATES

Soup dishes should be cleared in different stages due to the weight and appearance.

Clear the first set (flat plate, deep plate and large spoon) with your left hand.

Leave your ring and little finger free.

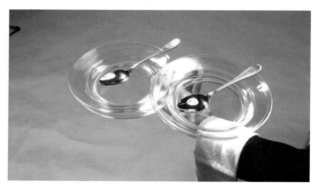

Clear the second set (flat plate, deep plate and large spoon) and place it on your thumb, ring finger and little finger, with your wrist protected by a cloth.

Take the large spoon from the top deep plate and place it in the bottom deep plate.

Take the deep plate with the two large spoons and place them in the top deep plate.

Clear a third set (flat plate, deep plate and large spoon) and place it on the bottom plate.

Take the large spoon from the top deep plate and place it in the bottom deep plate.

Take the deep plate with the three large spoons and place them in the top deep plate.

Continue clearing the table applying the method above.

HOLDING TWO PLATES AND A SAUCE BOAT

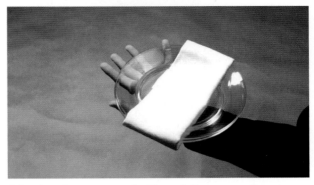

Take the plates covered with a cloth on your thumb, little finger and wrist.

Leave your index, middle and ring finger completely free.

Place the meat dish on a cloth covering the plates.

Place the dessert plate on your thumb and little finger, holding it with your index, middle and ring finger.

The other hand should stay free to carry the vegetable dish.

SERVICES METHODS

SERVICE	METHOD	
PLATE		
CLOCHE AND SERVING DISH		
FRENCH		
ENGLISH		
GUERIDON (RUSSIAN)		

CONCEPT	ADVANTAGES	DISADVANTAGES
The plates are prepared in the kitchen. The waiter brings them into the room and places them in front of the clients in order of precedence.	Relatively quick service (small tables). Dishes can be served warm. Does not require 'very qualified' staff.	Many staff members are required for large tables.
The plates are prepared in the kitchen. The waiter places them on a serving dish (silver), covers them with a cloche and brings the serving dish to the clients' table (on the gueridon). They then place the plates in front of each client and lift the cloche.	Dishes can be served warm. Grand and spectacular service (top-end restaurant).	Substantial investment in equipment required. Cannot be employed for large tables.
The service dish is accompanied by service cutlery and presented to the left of each client, who then serve themselves.	Little effort required of the staff. Does not require 'very qualified' staff.	Not very common in restaurants. Often employed in private houses or for old-fashioned banquets. Clients may sometimes struggle to serve themselves. The serving dish needs to be rearranged for the last portions.
Same concept as the French service but the waiter carries it out.	Quick service, often used for banquets.	Experienced staff with good dexterity required.
The plates are served on the gueridon placed in front of the clients' table. Service mainly employed in top-end restaurants for carving/slicing and flambéing.	Service can be used for all dishes. The waiter uses both hands and can neaten the presentation of the plates. Spectacular effect for carving/slicing and flambéing.	Slower than the English service. Greater investment in equipment and qualified staff required.

＊ **"One measure*"**
where indicated, is equivalent to **4 cl**.

COCKTAILS

DEFINITION

Drink mixes that can be prepared in three different ways: using a shaker, mixing glass or poured directly into the serving glass.

DIFFERENT CATEGORIES

BUCKS
Drinks based on lemon juice and ice, topped up with sparkling water.

COBBLERS
Low-alcohol drinks based on wine or diluted spirits, served with ice and garnished with seasonal fruit.

COOLERS
Low-alcohol drinks topped up with sparkling water.

CRUSTAS
Drinks based on spirits and lemon juice.

CUPS
Drinks based on spirits, liqueurs or wines, garnished with fruit, vegetables or other ingredients

DAISIES
Drinks based on spirits, lemon juice and orgeat syrup.

EGGNOGS
Drinks based on spirits and egg (yolk or whole); can be served hot or cold.

FIXES
Drinks based on lemon juice, spirits and sugar, topped up with sparkling water.

FIZZES
Drinks based on lemon juice, spirits, egg white and sparkling water.

FLIPS
Drinks based on spirits, liqueur or wine and egg; usually served cold.

HIGH-BALLS
Drinks with plenty of ice cubes, topped up generously with sparkling water.

HOT DRINKS
Hot drinks served in handle or stemmed glasses.

JULEPS
Drinks based on fresh mint.

LONG DRINKS
Low alcohol drinks with plenty of ice cubes, usually topped up with sparkling water, tonic, etc.

MULLS
Hot drinks based on wine.

POUSSE L'AMOUR
Drinks based on egg yolks, liqueur and spices.

PUNCHES
Hot or cold drinks based on lemon juice, fruit juice and spirits.

RYEKYS
Low-sugar drinks based on spirits and lemon juice, topped up with sparkling water.

SANGAREES
Drinks based on spirits and nutmeg (can be topped up with beer).

SCHRUBS
Variety of brewed fruit drinks.

SHORT DRINKS
High-alcohol drinks served in small glasses.

SLINGS
Hot or cold drinks based on spirits, lemon juice and sugar (or syrup).

SMASHES
Refreshing drinks based on fresh mint and spirits.

SOURS
Sour drinks based on lemon juice (very dry fizz).

STRAIGHT
All drinks served on their own, natural, on ice.

SWIZZIE
Drinks accompanied by a swizzle stick.

TODDIES
Drinks based on spirits or liqueur, sugar and flavoured with Angostura.

COCKTAIL BAR EQUIPMENT

A: Shaker. **B:** Measures. **C:** Soda water (syphon). **D:** Ice bucket. **E:** Sugar dish.
F: Strainer (cocktail strainer). **G:** Mixing glass. **H:** Nutmeg grater. **I:** Citrus fruit knife. **J:** Mixing spoon.
K: Ice spoon. **L:** Sugar tongs.

ITEMS NEEDED

ALASKA

Shaker, strainer, cocktail glass, ice bucket, ice spoon, yellow Izarra, gin.

The Izarra can be replaced by yellow Chartreuse.

ALEXANDER

Shaker, strainer, cocktail glass, ice bucket, ice spoon, crème fraîche, brown crème de cacao, cognac.

BACARDI

Shaker, strainer, cocktail glass, ice bucket, ice spoon, grenadine syrup, lemon juice, Ron Bacardi.

COCKTAILS

Fill the shaker with $\frac{2}{3}$ ice.
$\frac{3}{10}$ yellow Izarra (or yellow Chartreuse).
$\frac{7}{10}$ gin.
Shake and strain into a cocktail glass.

Fill the shaker with $\frac{2}{3}$ ice.
1 teaspoon of crème fraîche.
$\frac{2}{10}$ brown crème de cacao.
$\frac{7}{10}$ cognac.
Shake and strain into a cocktail glass.

Fill the shaker with $\frac{2}{3}$ ice.
$\frac{1}{10}$ grenadine syrup.
$\frac{3}{10}$ lemon juice.
$\frac{6}{10}$ Ron Bacardi.
Shake and strain into a cocktail glass.

BRONX

Shaker, strainer, cocktail glass, ice bucket, ice spoon, orange juice, dry vermouth, Italian vermouth, gin.

Fill the shaker with ⅔ ice.
¹⁄₁₀ orange juice.
²⁄₁₀ dry vermouth.
²⁄₁₀ Italian vermouth.
⁵⁄₁₀ gin.
Shake and strain into a cocktail glass.

B AND B

A serving glass.
Bénédictine, brandy.

Strain directly into the serving glass.
⁵⁄₁₀ Bénédictine.
⁵⁄₁₀ brandy.

BLACK RUSSIAN

"Old Fashioned" glass, ice bucket, ice spoon, coffee liqueur, vodka.

Fill the "Old Fashioned" glass with ice.
Strain directly:
³⁄₁₀ coffee liqueur.
⁷⁄₁₀ vodka.

CHAMPAGNE COCKTAIL

Champagne flute, sugar cubes, Angostura bitters, cognac, champagne.

Put ¼ of a sugar cube soaked in Angostura bitters in the bottom of the champagne flute.
1 dash of cognac.
Top up with champagne.
Garnish.

CLOVER CLUB

Shaker, strainer, cocktail glass, ice bucket, ice spoon, egg, grenadine syrup, lemon juice, gin.

Fill the shaker with ⅔ ice.
½ egg white.
¹⁄₁₀ grenadine syrup.
³⁄₁₀ lemon juice.
⁶⁄₁₀ gin.
Shake and strain into a cocktail glass.

DAIQUIRI

Shaker, strainer, cocktail glass, ice bucket, ice spoon, cane sugar syrup, lemon juice, white rum.

Fill the shaker with ⅔ ice.
¹⁄₁₀ cane sugar syrup.
³⁄₁₀ lemon juice.
⁶⁄₁₀ white rum.
Shake and strain into a cocktail glass.

DUBONNET COCKTAIL

Mixing glass, strainer, mixing spoon, ice bucket, cocktail glass, Dubonnet, gin.

Strain into the mixing glass:
$^5/_{10}$ Dubonnet.
$^5/_{10}$ gin.
Add $^1/_3$ ice.
Mix and strain into a cocktail glass.

GIBSON

Mixing glass, strainer, mixing spoon, cocktail glass, ice bucket, ice spoon, dry vermouth, gin, cocktail onions.

Strain into the mixing glass:
$^2/_{10}$ dry vermouth.
$^8/_{10}$ gin.
Add $^1/_3$ ice.
Mix and strain into a cocktail glass.
Add 1 or 2 cocktail onions.

GRASSHOPPER

Shaker, strainer, cocktail glass, ice bucket, ice spoon, crème fraîche, white crème de cacao, green crème de menthe.

Fill the shaker with $^2/_3$ ice.
1 spoon of crème fraîche.
$^3/_{10}$ white crème de cacao.
$^7/_{10}$ green crème de menthe.
Shake and strain into a cocktail glass.

TEQUILA SUNRISE

Shaker, strainer, cocktail glass, ice bucket, ice spoon, orange juice, tequila, grenadine syrup.

Fill the shaker with ⅔ ice.
⁶⁄₁₀ orange juice.
⁴⁄₁₀ tequila.
Shake and strain into a cocktail glass.
Finish with a dash of grenadine.

JACK ROSE

Shaker, strainer, cocktail glass, ice bucket, ice spoon, grenadine syrup, lemon juice, Calvados.

Fill the shaker with ⅔ ice.
¹⁄₁₀ grenadine syrup.
³⁄₁₀ lemon juice.
⁶⁄₁₀ Calvados.
Shake and strain into a cocktail glass.

MANHATTAN

Mixing glass, strainer, mixing spoon, ice bucket, ice spoon, cocktail glass, Angostura bitters, Italian vermouth, bourbon, cherry.

Strain into the mixing glass.
Several drops of Angostura bitters.
³⁄₁₀ Italian vermouth.
⁷⁄₁₀ bourbon.
Add ⅓ ice.
Mix and strain into a cocktail glass.
Add a cherry.

MARGARITA

Shaker, strainer, cocktail glass, ice bucket, ice spoon, lemon juice, Cointreau, tequila.

Fill the shaker with ⅔ ice.
¹⁄₁₀ lemon juice.
³⁄₁₀ Cointreau.
⁶⁄₁₀ tequila.
Shake and strain into a cocktail glass - with a salt rim if desired.

DRY MARTINI

Mixing glass, strainer, mixing spoon, ice bucket, ice spoon, cocktail glass, dry vermouth, gin.

Strain into the mixing glass.
²⁄₁₀ dry vermouth.
⁸⁄₁₀ gin.
Add ⅔ ice.
Mix and strain into a cocktail glass.

SCOTCH OLD FASHIONED

"Old Fashioned" glass, ice bucket, ice spoon, sugar cubes, sugar tongs, Angostura bitters, scotch whisky, orange, lemon, cherry.

Crush ¼ of a sugar cube soaked in Angostura bitters in an "Old Fashioned" glass.
Fill with ice.
Add one measure* of scotch.
Stir and garnish with the orange, lemon and cherry.

ORANGE BLOSSOM

Shaker, strainer, cocktail glass, ice bucket, ice spoon, orange juice, gin.

Fill the shaker with ⅔ ice.
⁶⁄₁₀ orange juice.
⁴⁄₁₀ gin.
Shake and strain into a cocktail glass.

PARADISE

Shaker, strainer, cocktail glass, ice bucket, ice spoon, orange juice, apricot brandy, gin.

Fill the shaker with ⅔ ice.
¹⁄₁₀ orange juice.
³⁄₁₀ apricot brandy.
⁶⁄₁₀ gin.
Shake and strain into a cocktail glass.

PINK GIN

Cocktail glass, Angostura bitters, gin.

Swirl two dashes of Angostura bitters in a cocktail glass.
Strain in a measure* of gin.
Serve with a glass of water with ice.

PINK LADY

Shaker, strainer, cocktail glass, ice bucket, ice spoon, grenadine syrup, lemon juice, gin.

Fill the shaker with ⅔ ice.
¹⁄₁₀ grenadine syrup.
³⁄₁₀ lemon juice.
⁶⁄₁₀ gin.
Shake and strain into a cocktail glass.

RUSTY NAIL

Ice bucket, ice spoon, "Old Fashioned" glass, scotch whisky liqueur, scotch whisky.

Fill the "Old Fashioned" glass with ice.
⁵⁄₁₀ scotch whisky liqueur.
⁵⁄₁₀ scotch whisky.

ROB ROY

Mixing glass, strainer, mixing spoon, cocktail glass, ice bucket, ice spoon, Angostura bitters, Italian vermouth, scotch whisky, cherry.

Strain into the mixing glass.
Several drops of Angostura bitters.
²⁄₁₀ Italian vermouth.
⁸⁄₁₀ scotch whisky.
⅓ ice.
Mix and strain into a cocktail glass.
Add a cherry.

ROSE

Mixing glass, strainer, mixing spoon, cocktail glass, ice bucket, ice spoon, dry vermouth, kirsch, cherry brandy, cherry.

Strain into the mixing glass.
6/10 dry vermouth.
2/10 kirsch.
2/10 cherry brandy.
1/3 ice.
Mix and strain into a cocktail glass.
Add a cherry.

RED LION

Shaker, strainer, cocktail glass, ice bucket, ice spoon, orange juice, lemon juice, Grand Marnier, gin.

Fill the shaker with 2/3 ice.
2/10 orange juice.
2/10 lemon juice.
3/10 Grand Marnier.
3/10 gin.
Shake and strain into a cocktail glass.

SIDE-CAR

Shaker, strainer, cocktail glass, ice bucket, ice spoon, lemon juice, Cointreau, cognac.

Fill the shaker with 2/3 ice.
1/10 lemon juice.
3/10 Cointreau.
6/10 cognac.
Shake and strain into a cocktail glass.

STINGER

Shaker, strainer, cocktail glass, ice bucket, ice spoon, white crème de menthe, cognac.

Fill the shaker with ⅔ ice.
³⁄₁₀ white crème de menthe.
⁷⁄₁₀ cognac.
Shake and strain into a cocktail glass.

SUISSESSE

Shaker, strainer, tumbler, ice bucket, ice spoon, syphon, egg, lemon juice, Pernod.

Fill the shaker with ⅔ ice.
¹⁄₁₀ egg white.
³⁄₁₀ lemon juice.
⁷⁄₁₀ Pernod.
Shake and strain into a tumbler.
Top up with soda.

TRINITY

Mixing glass, strainer, mixing spoon, ice bucket, ice spoon, cocktail glass, dry vermouth, Italian vermouth, gin.

Strain into the mixing glass:
³⁄₁₀ dry vermouth.
³⁄₁₀ Italian vermouth.
⁴⁄₁₀ gin.
Add ⅓ ice.
Mix and strain into a cocktail glass.
Squeeze in a few drops of lemon.

WHITE LADY

Shaker, strainer, cocktail glass, ice bucket, ice spoon, lemon juice, Cointreau, gin.

Fill the shaker with ⅔ ice.
¹⁄₁₀ lemon juice.
³⁄₁₀ Cointreau.
⁶⁄₁₀ gin.
Shake and strain into a cocktail glass.

TOM COLLINS

Ice bucket, ice spoon, tumbler, syphon, caster sugar, lemon juice, gin, lemon, cherry.

Fill the tumbler with ice.
Add 1 teaspoon of caster sugar,
⁵⁄₁₀ lemon juice,
⁵⁄₁₀ gin.
Top up with soda.
Garnish with a slice of lemon and a cherry.

GIN FIZZ

Shaker, strainer, tumbler, syphon, ice bucket, ice spoon, caster sugar, lemon juice, gin.

Fill the shaker with ⅔ ice.
Add 1 teaspoon of caster sugar.
⁵⁄₁₀ lemon juice.
⁵⁄₁₀ gin.
Shake and strain into a tumbler.
Top up with soda.

GOLDEN FIZZ

Shaker, strainer, tumbler, syphon, ice bucket, ice spoon, egg, caster sugar, lemon juice, gin.

Fill the shaker with ⅔ ice.
1 egg yolk.
Add 1 teaspoon of caster sugar.
⁵⁄₁₀ lemon juice.
⁵⁄₁₀ gin.
Shake and strain into a tumbler.
Top up with soda.

SILVER FIZZ

Shaker, strainer, tumbler, syphon, ice bucket, ice spoon, egg, caster sugar, lemon juice, gin.

Fill the shaker with ⅔ ice.
1 egg white.
Add 1 teaspoon of caster sugar.
⁵⁄₁₀ lemon juice.
⁵⁄₁₀ gin.
Shake and strain into a tumbler.
Top up with soda.

PORTO FLIP

Shaker, strainer, cocktail glass, ice bucket, ice spoon, egg, caster sugar, cognac, red Port, nutmeg grater, nutmeg.

Fill the shaker with ⅔ ice.
1 egg yolk.
Add 1 teaspoon of caster sugar.
2 dashes of cognac.
1 measure* of red Port.
Shake and strain into a cocktail glass.
Dust with nutmeg.

PLANTER'S PUNCH

Tumbler, ice bucket, ice spoon, orange Curaçao, Maraschino, lemon juice, orange juice, pineapple juice, white rum, dark rum, pineapple, cherries.

Fill the tumbler with ice.
1 dash of orange Curaçao.
1 dash of Maraschino.
²⁄₁₀ lemon juice.
²⁄₁₀ orange juice.
²⁄₁₀ pineapple juice.
⁴⁄₁₀ white rum.
Stir, add a dash of dark rum.
Garnish with a quarter-slice of pineapple and 2 cherries.

SCOTCH SOUR

Shaker, strainer, cocktail glass, ice bucket, ice spoon, caster sugar, lemon juice, scotch whisky.

Fill the shaker with ⅔ ice.
Add 1 teaspoon of caster sugar.
³⁄₁₀ lemon juice.
⁷⁄₁₀ scotch whisky.
Shake and strain into a cocktail glass.

SINGAPORE SLING

Shaker, strainer, tumbler, ice bucket, ice spoon, syphon, lemon juice, gin, cherry brandy.

Fill the shaker with ⅔ ice.
²⁄₁₀ lemon juice.
⁴⁄₁₀ gin.
⁴⁄₁₀ cherry brandy.
Shake and strain into a tumbler.
Top up with soda (or still water).

AMERICANO

Tumbler, ice bucket, ice spoon, syphon, Campari Bitter, Italian vermouth, orange, lemon.

Fill the tumbler with ice.
⁷⁄₁₀ Campari Bitter.
³⁄₁₀ Italian vermouth.
Add a little soda.
Garnish with 1 slice of orange and ½ slice of lemon.

BARBOTTAGE

Shaker, strainer, champagne flute, ice bucket, ice spoon, grenadine syrup, lemon juice, orange juice, champagne.

Fill the shaker with ⅔ ice.
¹⁄₁₀ grenadine syrup.
³⁄₁₀ lemon juice.
⁶⁄₁₀ orange juice.
Shake and strain into a champagne flute.
Top up with champagne.

TAMPICO

Tumbler, ice bucket, ice spoon, lemon juice, Campari, Cointreau, tonic.

Fill the tumbler with ice.
³⁄₁₀ lemon juice.
⁴⁄₁₀ Campari.
³⁄₁₀ Cointreau.
Top up with tonic.

BLOODY MARY

Tumbler, ice bucket, ice spoon, celery salt, Tabasco, Worcestershire sauce, lemon juice, vodka, tomato juice.

Fill the tumbler with ice.
1 dash of Tabasco.
1 dash of Worcestershire sauce.
¹⁄₁₀ lemon juice.
³⁄₁₀ vodka.
⁶⁄₁₀ tomato juice.
Dust with celery salt and stir.

BRANDY EGGNOG

Shaker, strainer, tumbler, ice bucket, ice spoon, nutmeg grater, nutmeg, caster sugar, egg, cognac, milk.

Fill the shaker with ⅔ ice.
Add 1 teaspoon of caster sugar.
1 egg yolk.
1 measure* of cognac.
Shake and strain into a tumbler.
Top up with milk
Dust with nutmeg.

MACCA

Tumbler, ice bucket, ice spoon, crème de cassis, dry vermouth, Italian vermouth, gin.

Fill the tumbler with ice.
¹⁄₁₀ crème de cassis.
³⁄₁₀ dry vermouth.
³⁄₁₀ Italian vermouth.
³⁄₁₀ gin.
Add a little soda.

NEGRONI

Tumbler, ice bucket, ice spoon, Italian vermouth, Campari Bitter, gin, orange, lemon.

Fill the tumbler with ice.
³⁄₁₀ Italian vermouth.
³⁄₁₀ Campari Bitter.
⁴⁄₁₀ gin.
Garnish with 1 slice of orange and 1 slice of lemon.

PIMM'S N°1

"Long drink" cocktail glass, ice bucket, ice spoon, Pimm's, soda, orange, lemon, cherry.

Fill the "long drink' cocktail glass with ice.
Strain 1 measure* of Pimm's.
Top up with soda.
Garnish with 1 slice of orange, 1 slice of lemon and a cherry.

SCREWDRIVER

Tumbler, ice bucket, ice spoon, vodka, orange juice.

Fill the tumbler with ice.
$^4/_{10}$ vodka.
$^6/_{10}$ orange juice.

BEVERAGES SERVICES

SERVING RED WINE

IMPORTANT

- Hold the bottle in your right hand, without hiding the label, with the neck over the wine glass.
- Pour gently.
- Keep your left hand, holding the cloth, behind your back.
- After pouring each glass, discretely wipe the neck with the cloth to prevent any drops falling on the tablecloth, or client!

"
- The cloth may be placed under the neck.
- Red wine should be uncorked on the guéridon in front of the clients' table.

METHOD

Present the bottle to the client with the label facing them so that they can check the appellation and vintage of the wine ordered.

Cut the foil capsule under the rim of the neck around half of the circumference using a corkscrew knife.

Continue cutting the capsule around the other half of the circumference.

Remove the capsule using the corkscrew knife.

Place it in the plate for waste.

Wipe the neck and cork with the cloth.

Place the tip of the screw in the centre of cork.

Push it in, without piercing right through as bits of the cork could fall in the wine.

Place the lip of the corkscrew knife on the edge of the neck.

Remove the cork very delicately, pulling upwards.

Your left hand should be holding the corkscrew knife lip tightly on the edge of the neck.

Finish removing the cork with your right hand and smell the wine immediately to check for suspicious odours (risk of spoilt wine).

Keep the cork on the decanter tray.

Before serving, wipe the neck of the bottle with your cloth.

SERVING WHITE WINE

IMPORTANT

- After having quickly wiped the bottle, hold it in your right hand, without hiding the label, with the neck over the wine glass.
- Pour gently.
- Keep your left hand, holding the cloth, behind your back.
- After pouring each glass, discretely wipe the neck with the cloth to prevent any drops falling on the tablecloth, or client!

METHOD

"

- White wine prepared in a wine bucket.
- Equipment needed: bucket, bottle, ice and water; add enough ice for the temperature required.
- White wine should be uncorked in the bucket in front of the clients' table. The bucket can be presented on a wine stand or a dessert plate on a guéridon.

Present the bottle to the client with the label facing them so that they can check the appellation and vintage of the wine ordered.

The cloth should be placed under the bottle.

Cut the foil capsule under the rim of the neck around half of the circumference using a corkscrew knife.

Continue cutting the capsule around the other half of the circumference.

Remove the capsule using the corkscrew knife.

Place it in the plate for waste.

Wipe the neck and cork with the cloth.

Place the tip of the screw in the centre of cork.

Push it in, without piercing right through as bits of the cork could fall in the wine.

Place the lip of the corkscrew knife on the edge of the neck.

Remove the cork very delicately, pulling upwards.

Your left hand should be holding the corkscrew knife lip tightly on the edge of the neck.

Finish removing the cork with your right hand and smell the wine immediately to check for suspicious odours (risk of spoilt wine).

Keep the cork on the decanter tray.

Before serving, wipe the neck of the bottle with your cloth.

DIFFERENT CAPSULE TYPES

Red wine with a "foil capsule".
Red wine with a "plastic capsule".

For red wines with a "plastic capsule", cut **above** the glass rim (pre-cut capsules). There is no risk of oxidation for these bottles and it would therefore be difficult to cut below the rim. The plastic capsule may be fully removed.

White wine with a "foil capsule".
White wine with a "plastic capsule".

For white wines with a "plastic capsule", cut **above** the glass rim (pre-cut capsules). There is no risk of oxidation for these bottles and it would therefore be difficult to cut below the rim. The plastic capsule may be fully removed.

PRESENTATION OF DIFFERENT SERVING BUCKETS

"1/2 bottle" bucket. "Bottle" or "Champagne" bucket. "Magnum" (1,5L bottle) bucket. "Rhine wine" bucket.

SERVING CHAMPAGNE

IMPORTANT

- After having wiped the bottle, hold it in your right hand, without hiding the label, with the neck over the champagne flute.
- Pour gently and carefully.
- Keep your left hand, holding the cloth, behind your back.
- After pouring each flute, discretely wipe the neck with the cloth to prevent any drops falling on the tablecloth, or client!

- Champagne prepared in a champagne bucket with as much ice as possible.
- Equipment: bucket, bottle, ice, water.

METHOD

Present the bottle to the client with the label facing them so that they can check the appellation and vintage of the champagne ordered.
The cloth should be placed under the bottle.

Remove the foil casing while holding the cork in tightly with your left thumb.

Remove the metal muselet while holding the cork in place.
Make sure you hold your thumb on the cork.

Carefully remove the cork, holding the bottle tightly in the bucket with your left hand.

SERVING A CHAMPAGNE MAGNUM

Take a magnum bottle in your right hand, with your thumb placed on the inside of the base.

Hold the neck above the champagne flute with the index finger of your left hand.

Pour very slowly.

SERVING RED WINE IN A POURING BASKET

IMPORTANT

- Hold the basket in your right hand with your index finger keeping the bottle in it.
- The neck should be positioned above the wine glass.
- Pour gently.

METHOD

- Make sure you put a napkin in the basket, under the bottleneck, to soak up wine drops while you serve.
- Red wine is served in a pouring basket on a guéridon in front of the client.
- Place a bread plate upside down under the pouring basket so that the bottle is lifted and the wine will not spill onto the tablecloth when you remove the cork.

Present the bottle to the client in its basket with the label facing them so that they can check the appellation and vintage of the wine ordered.

Cut the foil capsule under the rim of the neck around half of the circumference using a corkscrew knife.

Continue cutting the capsule around the other half of the circumference.

Remove the capsule using the corkscrew knife.
Place it in the upside-down bread plate.

Wipe the neck and cork with the cloth.

Place the tip of the screw in the centre of cork.
Push it in, without piercing right through as bits of the cork could fall in the wine.

Place the lip of the corkscrew knife on the edge of the neck.

Remove the cork very delicately, pulling upwards.
Your left hand should be holding the corkscrew knife lip tightly on the edge of the neck.

Finish removing the cork with your right hand and smell the wine immediately to check for suspicious odours (risk of spoilt wine).
Keep the cork on the upside-down bread plate.

Before serving, wipe the neck of the bottle with your cloth.

DECANTING

EQUIPMENT

Decanter
Waiter's corkscrew knife
Candle holder
Bread plate
Wine to be decanted presented in a serving basket

A decanter basket may be used.

METHOD

Present the bottle to the client in its basket with the label facing them so that they can check the appellation and vintage of the wine ordered.

Serving red wine in a decanter:

Hold the decanter in your right hand, with the spout positioned above the wine glass.

Pour gently.

Remove the "foil" capsule completely using the corkscrew knife. This will allow you to see the wine through the glass of the bottleneck shoulder.

Uncork the bottle applying the same method as used for serving red wine in a basket.

Light the candle.

Hold the decanter in your left hand.

Take the bottle in your right hand and hold it in front of the candle so that the flame lights up the bottle shoulders.

Pour the wine into the decanter.

Looking through the bottle shoulders, ensure that no sediment enters the decanter.

As soon as you see sediment, stop pouring.

SERVING SPIRITS AND LIQUEURS

WHITES SPIRITS

Whites spirits are usually served "chilled" but they should not be served so cold as to loose part of their flavour and bouquet.

Equipment and ingredients

- Whites spirits
- Ice bucket
- Ice spoon
- Tasting glass, saucer, little cloth.
- Saucer served with a little napkin.

Serving

- Put three ice cubes in the tasting glass.
- Swirl the ice cubes round to ice the glass.
- Turn the glass over onto the saucer and napkin and allow it to drip-dry for a few seconds.
- Serve the white spirits.
- Present the glass on the saucer with a little napkin.

WINE SPIRITS AND LIQUEURS

Wine spirits and liqueurs are not usually served iced, unless specifically requested by the client for certain liqueurs (Grand Marnier, Marie Brizard, etc.).

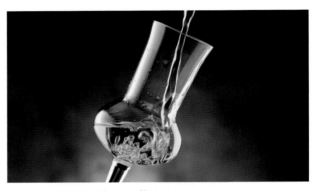

Equipment and ingredients

- Wine spirits or liqueurs
- Saucer
- Little cloth
- Tasting glass.

Serving

- Serve the wine spirit or liqueur in the tasting glass.
- Present the glass on the saucer with a little napkin.

SERVING HOT DRINKS

SERVING COFFEE

Serving coffee with a dessert, ideal for clients in a rush

Place the hot cup and saucer to the right of the dessert plate, with the teaspoon on the right side of the saucer.

Serve the coffee English-style or directly in the cup (coffee prepared by machine, for example).

Remember the sugar.

Serving coffee after clearing the dessert plates

Preparing the table.

Leave the following items on the table:

• water glasses and water jug (or bottle).

• Ash tray, floral decoration and table number.

Set a dessert plate, saucer and warm cup (handle to the left), teaspoon on the right and, not to be forgotten, the sugar.

Serving coffee

As for all drinks, coffee in a pot is served to the right of the client (with a saucer).

The coffee pot can be left on a warmer placed on the guéridon.

(Several coffee pots containing different coffee options may be served).

SERVING TEA

Preparing the table

Same preparation as for coffee.

Equipment

• Dessert plate

• Tea saucer

• Warm teacup

• Teaspoon

Ingredients

• Teapot filled with boiling water and a teabag

• Pot of hot water

• For tea: serve lemon slices on the saucer or a pot of milk if desired by the client.

• Sugar selection.

(Several teapots containing different teas may be served).

STARTERS

ARTICHOKE WITH VINAIGRETTE

GUÉRIDON

1 pair of tongs
2 dessert spoons
1 sauce boat on a plate
3 serving plates
1 deep plate to prepare the vinaigrette
1 plate for trimmings
3 artichokes
Salt, pepper, oil, vinegar

PRESENTATION

Artichokes and vinaigrette.

Sprinkle salt and pepper into the deep plate.
Pour in two large spoonfuls of vinegar.

Dissolve the salt and pepper in the vinegar with the back of the fork.

Add two large spoonfuls of oil.

Blend the oil and vinegar using the fork.

Add two large spoonfuls of oil.

Blend again using the fork.

Pour the vinaigrette into the sauce boat using the spoon.

Remove the heart and keep it to one side of the plate.

Remove the choke and the other little leaves using a dessert spoon. The artichoke can be held in place using a pair of tongs.

Remove the choke without damaging the heart. The artichoke can be held in place using a pincer.

AVOCADO AND PRAWNS

GUÉRIDON

1 pair of tongs
1 table knife
1 teaspoon
Cognac, ketchup
Worcestershire sauce, Tabasco
Pepper, salt, paprika (with a teaspoon)

½ lemon and a slice cut in two
2 dessert plates garnished with shredded lettuce
2 large spoonfuls of mayonnaise in a deep plate
100g of shelled prawns in a deep plate
1 avocado

PRESENTATION

Avocado and prawns.

Squeeze a lemon half over the mayonnaise by pricking the pulp with the fork and rotating it.

Add a few drops of Tabasco, a dash of Worcestershire sauce and sprinkle with paprika, salt and pepper.

Add a large spoonful of ketchup and mix.

Pour one centilitre of cognac in and mix.

Spoon the "cocktail" sauce over the prawns and mix again.

Hold the avocado in the palm of your hand with the stem facing upwards.

Cut the avocado in two starting from the stem to obtain two even parts.

Open the avocado, with the stone remaining on one side.

Hold the half avocado with the stone in the palm of your hand.

Hit the stone sharply with the edge of the knife blade and remove it without damaging the flesh.

Make the pit of the stone a little larger by removing some of the flesh with a teaspoon.

Mix this flesh with the prawns.

Place the avocado halves on the shredded lettuce.

Garnish with the prawns.

Decorate with half a slice of lemon dipped in paprika.

CAVIAR

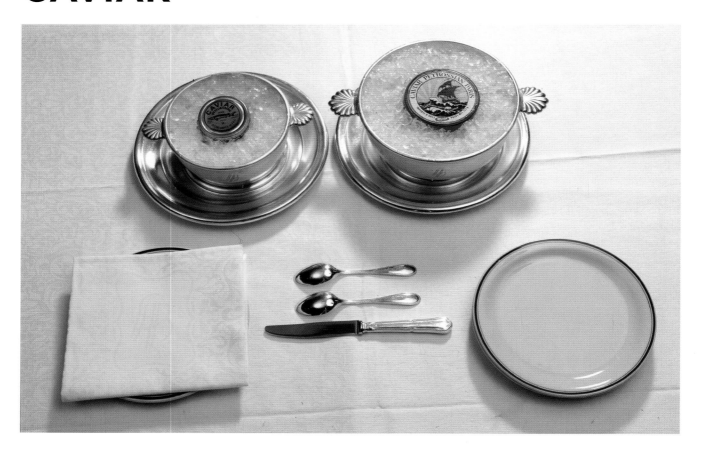

GUÉRIDON

2 teaspoons
1 dessert knife
1 napkin on a plate
2 serving plates

1 50g tin of "Sevruga" on a bed of crushed ice
1 125g tin of "Beluga XL" on a bed of crushed ice

PRESENTATION

Two different types of caviar:

• "SEVRUGA" caviar

• "BELUGA XL" caviar

Hold the pot using the napkin.

Slide the end of the blade between the glass and the edge of the lid to open the tin.

Place the tin with its lid back on the crushed ice.

Hold the tin using the napkin.

Slide the end of the blade under the rubber ring to remove it.

Place the rubber ring on the crushed ice.

Gently turn the lid to open it.

Place the tin with its lid back on the crushed ice.

Take a spoonful of caviar.

Serve it delicately on the plate using the other spoon.

COCKTAIL PRAWNS

GUÉRIDON

1 pair of tongs
Cognac
Ketchup
Worcestershire sauce
Tabasco
Pepper
Salt
Paprika (with a teaspoon)

2 coupes garnished with lettuce leaves, on a serving plate
½ lemon and a slice cut in two
4 dessert spoonfuls of mayonnaise in a deep plate
250 g of shelled prawns in a deep plate

PRESENTATION

Cocktail prawns.

Squeeze a lemon half over the mayonnaise by pricking the pulp with the fork and rotating it.

Add a large spoonful of ketchup and mix.

Add a few drops of Tabasco, one or two dashes of Worcestershire sauce, one centilitre of Cognac and salt and pepper, and mix well.

Coat the prawns with one or two spoonfuls of the "cocktail" sauce.

Ensure the sauce coats the prawns evenly.

Serve the prawns in the coupes.

Decorate each coupe with half a slice of lemon dipped in paprika.

Shredded lettuce is sometimes used as it makes the dish easier to eat.

FIGS

GUÉRIDON

1 spoon and 1 dessert plate
1 paring knife
1 preparation plate

1 plate for trimmings
2 presentation plates, figs on a plate

PRESENTATION

Figs.

Cut into the skin of the fig around the stem.

Make five to six incisions down its length.

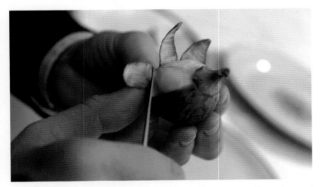

Peel the fruit, holding the skin between your thumb and the blade of the knife.

Hold the fig upright on the plate, holding it by the stem. Finish peeling the skin, cutting it if necessary.

Remove the fruit from the skin, holding it down with the knife.

Cut the stem.

Place the fig in the service plate and slice it with the help of a fork.

Fig and ham presentation.

FOIE GRAS

GUÉRIDON

1 pair of tongs
2 table knives
1 napkin
1 vegetable dish filled with boiling water
1 plate for the cutlery
1 dessert plate for the first slice
Serving plates

PRESENTATION

Three plates served with foie gras, the terrine and the first slice.

Dip the knife blade into the boiling water to heat it.

Wipe the blade on the napkin to remove the water.

Cut the first slice from left to right, holding the terrine firmly.

Loosen the first slice around the edges of the terrine dish.

Remove the first slice, holding it between the blades of both knives.
Place the first slice on the dessert plate.
Cut and serve three thin slices of foie gras per plate.

Carefully wipe the blade of the knife in the folded napkin after cutting each slice.

Dip the blade into the boiling water. (A real pot of water makes this easier)

Wipe the blade on the napkin.

Continue to cut thin slices.

Place the slices on the serving plates using the second knife.

FULL MELON

GUÉRIDON

1 pair of tongs
1 dessert spoon
1 melon baller
1 paring knife
2 serving plates

1 small salad bowl (for the melon balls)
1 preparation plate
1 plate for trimmings
2 "portion" melons

PRESENTATION

Melon on a plate and in a coupe with crushed ice.

Hold the melon upright on the plate.

Cut the cap in the shape of a four-leaf clover using the paring knife.

Remove the cap.

Remove the seeds in the cap.

Hold the melon above the deep plate.

Remove the seeds and the filaments using a dessert spoon.

Remove the seeds.

Hollow out the melon with the melon baller.

Place the melon balls in the small salad bowl.

Garnish the hollow melon with the melon balls using a pair of tongs.

The melon will soak up alcohol (port, for example) better if presented in balls.

MELON HALF

GUÉRIDON

1 pair of tongs
1 stainless steel slicing knife
2 serving plates

1 preparation plate
1 plate for trimmings
1 melon

PRESENTATION

Half melon on a plate and in a coupe with crushed ice.

Hold the melon side down on the preparation plate.
Cut the stem.

Rotate the melon.
Cut off a small base.

Cut the melon in two, perpendicular to the sides.

Hold the half melon above the deep plate.
Remove the seeds and the filaments using a spoon.

Remove the seeds and place them on the plate for trimmings.
Apply the same method to the other half.

MELON SLICES

GUÉRIDON

1 pair of tongs
1 paring knife
1 stainless steel slicing knife
2 serving plates
1 preparation plate
1 plate for trimmings
1 melon

PRESENTATION

Melon slices.

Hold the melon side down on the preparation plate.
Cut the stem.

Hold the melon upright on the preparation plate.
Cut the melon in line with the sides.

Hold the half melon above the deep plate.
Remove the seeds and the filaments using a spoon.

Remove the seeds.

Hold the half melon tilted on the preparation plate and cut a third.

Cut the remaining part in two.

Prick the skin at the edge of the slice.

Remove the skin using the paring knife.

Place the slices on the serving plate.

Italian-style melon presentation (with cured ham slices).

GRAPEFRUIT HALF

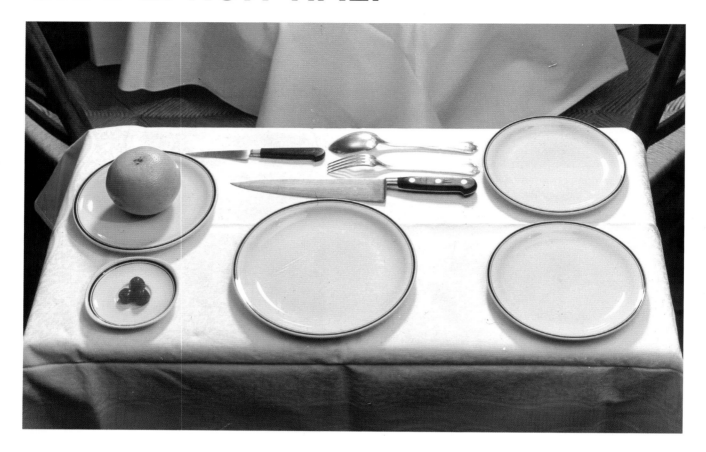

GUÉRIDON

1 pair of tongs
1 slicing knife
1 paring knife
2 serving plates

1 preparation plate
a few cherries in a saucer (for decoration)
1 grapefruit

PRESENTATION

Grapefruit:

• with a cherry in coupe on crushed ice (brought in last minute);

• without garnish on a dessert plate.

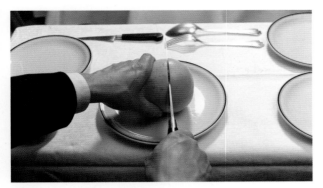

Hold the grapefruit on the preparation plate.

Cut the grapefruit in two, perpendicular to the supremes using a slicing knife.

Hold the grapefruit half on the preparation plate.

Remove the seeds using the tip of the knife.

Cut around the core to remove it.

Cut along the membranes separating the supremes from the centre outwards.

Cut between the supremes and the skin.

Cut and lift the supreme towards the centre to loosen it.

Lift each supreme as you continue to ensure they are all loose.

COCKTAIL GRAPEFRUIT

GUÉRIDON

1 pair of tongs
1 paring knife
1 serving plate

1 preparation plate
1 plate for trimmings
1 grapefruit (dotted line marking the incision)

PRESENTATION

Grapefruit supremes:

• in a coupe;

• with juice on a plate.

Hold the grapefruit on the deep plate.

Cut around the stem following the dotted line using the paring knife.

Rotate the grapefruit.

Cut a cap off the opposite end to the stem.

Prick the cap and push the prongs of the fork in completely.

Prick the stem side of the fruit and push the prongs of the fork in completely.

Peel the grapefruit quickly by cutting little slices of skin off.

Cut out the supremes between each membrane, above the preparation plate in order to salvage the juice.

SPAGHETTI NAPOLITANA

GUÉRIDON

1 pair of tongs
1 dessert knife
3 dessert spoons
2 warm deep plates
2 large plates
1 stove with a dessert plate

1 thick dish or bi-metal pan (optimal heat transmission)
20g butter
1 sauce boat of chopped tomatoes
1 sauce boat of tomato sauce
1 sauce boat of parmesan
1 vegetable dish of spaghetti (two portions)

PRESENTATION

Spaghetti Napolitana.

Turn on the stove.
Place the butter in the dish to melt.

Wrap the spaghetti around the fork prongs holding them with the spoon and place them in the dish.

Add salt and pepper to the spaghetti.
Coat the spaghetti in the butter while stretching them out.

Add half of the chopped tomatoes and all of the tomato sauce.

Sprinkle parmesan on to the client's desire.

Mix the spaghetti while stretching them.

Wrap small nests of the spaghetti and serve them on the warm deep plate.
Garnish with chopped tomatoes and parmesan.

For the second plate, serve the remaining spaghetti in one wrap.
Garnish with chopped tomatoes and parmesan.

CHARCUTERIE

CURED HAM

GUÉRIDON

1 pair of tongs
1 boning knife
1 hollow blade carving knife
1 napkin
1 plate for trimmings
Serving plates

1 ham holder
1 ham to the right (clamped to the holder, with the cushion facing upwards and the shank turned to the side of the clamp handles)

PRESENTATION

Steps of carving a cured ham:

• three plates of slices from the different parts of the cushion;

• a plate of slices carved from the stifle.

Hold the ham at the shank using the napkin.

Use the boning knife to remove enough rind for the number of portions to be served.

Trim some of the fat using the boning knife.

Cut thin slices using the carving knife.

Serve on the plate.

Using the boning knife, keep trimming the fat as you remove slices.

Continue carving almost until the bone appears.

Rotate the shank.

Carve almost right down to the bone.

Finish boning.

Remove the bone and place it on the plate for trimmings.

Rotate the shank. Continue to cut thin slices using the carving knife.

Gradually plate the slices by unfolding them onto the serving plates and spreading them out evenly.

Continue carving until you reach the femur.

Return the ham to the holder with the cushion facing upwards and the shank turned to the side of the clamp handles.

Remove the rind and fat as before.

Carve thin slices until the small bone appears.

Trim around the small bone using the boning knife. Remove the small bone and place it on the plate for trimmings. Continue cutting thin slices until you reach the femur.

YORK HAM

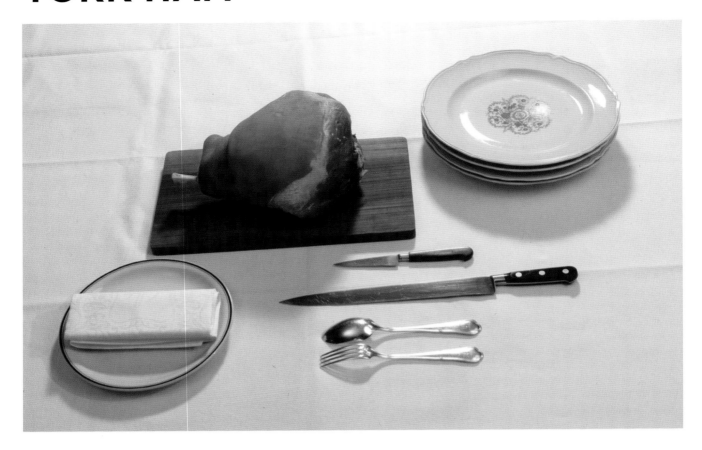

GUÉRIDON

1 pair of tongs
1 carving knife
1 paring knife
1 plate for trimmings
1 napkin
Serving plates
1 chopping board
1 York ham

PRESENTATION

York ham; portions obtained from different stages of carving.

Hold the ham flat on the board using the napkin.
Mark the heel of the ham using the carving knife.

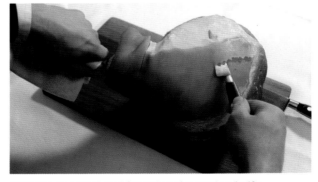

Remove the rind and fat using the paring knife.

Start cutting at an angle using the carving knife, 3-4 centimetres from the heel.

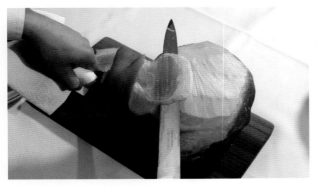

Begin cutting thin slices.

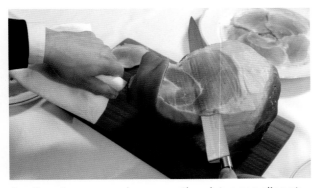

Continue to carve and serve on the plates one slice at a time.

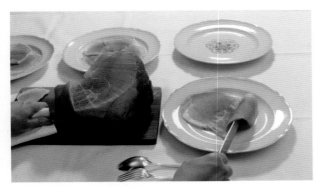

Plate the ham by unfolding the slices.

Carve until the bone.

Rotate the ham.
Remove the rind and fat using the paring knife.
Start cutting at an angle using the carving knife.

Cut thin slices and plate.

Carve until the bone.

PICKLED BEEF TONGUE, SALAMI, DRIED SAUSAGE, ANDOUILLE DE GUÉMÉNÉ, PÂTÉ EN CROÛTE, TERRINE

GUÉRIDON

1 pair of tongs
1 table knife
1 paring knife
1 slicing knife
1 carving knife

1 chopping board
1 table napkin
1 plate for trimmings
Serving plates
1 pickled beef tongue

1 country terrine
1 pâté en croûte
1 dried sausage
1 Andouille de Guéméné
1 salami

PRESENTATION

Cured meat buffet and four served plates.

Hold the tongue on its side using the napkin.
Cut the first part off at the 'throat side'.

Cut thin slices, following the curve of the tongue.

Hold the slices with the back on the spoon.
Remove the skin using the prongs of the fork.
Place on the serving plates.

Hold the salami on the board using the napkin.
Cut the first slice off using the carving knife.

Score the skin using the paring knife along the length and around the circumference of the salami according to the number of slices required.

Slide the blade of the paring knife under the skin along the incision.
Keep the skin on the blade using your thumb and peel it off.

Cut thin slices using the carving knife.
Place on the serving plates.

Hold the sausage flat on the board by using the napkin.
Cut the first part off diagonally in order to obtain larger slices.

Score the skin using the paring knife along the length and around the circumference of the sausage according to the number of slices required.

Slide the blade of the paring knife under the skin along the incision.

Keep the skin on the blade using your thumb and peel it off.

Cut thin slices using the carving knife.

Place on the serving plates.

Hold the Andouille de Guémené on the board using the napkin.

Cut the first part off diagonally in order to obtain larger slices.

Cut thin slices using the carving knife.

Hold the slices with the back on the spoon.

Remove the skin using the prongs of the fork.

Place on the serving plates.

Hold the pâté en croûte flat on the chopping board using the fork.

Cut the first part off using the slicing knife. Cut roughly 1cm-thick slices.

Place on the serving plates.

Hold the terrine.
Cut the first slice out and remove it using a table knife.

Remove the first slice using a table knife and fork.

Cut roughly 1cm-thick slices.

Remove the slices by holding them between the knife's blade and back of the fork.

SHELLFISH

LOBSTER

GUÉRIDON

1 pair of tongs
1 nutcracker
1 lobster pick
1 slicing knife
1 paring knife

1 chopping board
1 plate for trimmings
1 napkin
2 cold serving plates
1 lobster

PRESENTATION

Lobster (two plates).

Slide the fork under the claws and the spoon under the curve of the abdomen.

Place the lobster on the board.

Hold the lobster by the abdomen using the napkin.

Cut off the claws under the thorax and place them back in the dish.

Cut the legs off on each side and place them back in the dish.

Rotate the lobster and hold it by the thorax.

Cut into the thorax using the slicing knife.

Cut the abdomen in half in one sharp movement.

Rotate the lobster and hold the abdomen using the napkin.

Cut the thorax in half in one sharp movement.

Fully separate the two halves of the lobster.

Remove the intestine using the fork and spoon.

Remove the grey parts of the thorax using the spoon.

Prick the abdomen lobster meat using the fork.

Slide the spoon between the meat and the shell near the tail.

Remove the meat.

Place on the serving plate.

Hold the thorax using the fork.

Slide the spoon between the gills and shell to remove them.

Prick the inner thorax using the fork.

Remove the gills and place them on the plate for trimmings.

Place the inner thorax on the serving plate.

Cut the outer part of the legs off and place them on the plate for trimmings. You may use your fingers for the claws.

Hold the leg and cut the shell on each side using the paring knife.

Break the leg in two where you made the incision.

Remove the two parts of the shell to obtain the meat.

Place on the serving plate.

Hold the claw flat on the plate using the napkin.
Cut the joint near the claw using the slicing knife.

Break the shell at the joint using the nutcracker.
Place on the serving plate.

Hold the claw flat on the plate using the napkin.
Cut the shell on each side using the tip of the slicing knife.

Hold the claw using the napkin.
Dislocate the small pincer to obtain the meat.

Hold the claw flat on the board.
Break the claw shell by hitting it once sharply with the bolster of the slicing knife.
Remove the shell of the large pincer.

Hold the pincer meat using the flat blade of the knife.
Remove the claw shell to obtain the meat. Serve the claw meat.

FLAT AND CUPPED OYSTERS & MUSSELS

GUÉRIDON

1 oyster knife
1 paring knife
1 deep plate
1 kitchen towel
1 hamper of cupped oysters (Fine de Claire)
1 hamper of flat oysters (Belon)
1 dish of Spanish mussels
1 seafood platter garnished with crushed ice and seaweed.

PRESENTATION

Oyster & mussels platter.

Hold the oyster in the palm of your hand using the kitchen towel, with the flat shell facing upwards and the hinge facing you.

Insert the tip of the oyster knife between the two shells at the muscle side.

Push the blade 2-3 centimetres in.
Sever the abductor muscle.

Scrape the inside of the upper shell using the blade to remove the flesh.

Open the oyster without damaging the flesh.

Place the open oyster on the platter.

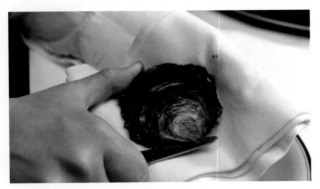

Hold the oyster with the kitchen towel, with the flat shell facing upwards and the opposite side to the hinge facing you.

Place the tip of the oyster knife between the two shells at the hinge side.

Sever the hinge and push the knife blade under the lid, without damaging the flesh, to cut the abductor muscle.

Sever the abductor muscle.

Scrape the inside of the upper shell using the blade to remove the flesh.

Open the oyster without damaging the flesh.

Place the open oyster on the platter.

Hold the shell between your index fingers and thumbs, above the deep plate.

Slide one shell on top of the other to allow the paring knife tip to enter.

Enter the paring knife tip at the abductor muscle side and sever it.

Scrape the inside of the upper shell to remove the flesh.

Open the mussels, sever the hinge ligaments to remove the upper shell.

SPINY LOBSTER

GUÉRIDON

1 pair of tongs
1 nutcracker
1 lobster pick
1 paring knife
1 slicing knife
1 chopping board
1 napkin
1 plate for trimmings
2 cold serving plates
1 spiny lobster

PRESENTATION

Spiny lobster (two plates).

Slide the spoon and fork under the thorax.
Place the lobster on the board.

Hold the lobster by the thorax using the napkin.
Cut into the thorax using the slicing knife.

Cut the abdomen in half in one sharp movement.

Rotate the spiny lobster and hold the abdomen using the napkin.
Cut the thorax in half in one sharp movement.

Fully separate the two halves of spiny lobster.

Cut the antenna.

Split the antenna in two along its length.

Remove the intestine using the fork and spoon.

Prick the abdomen lobster meat using the fork.
Slide the spoon between the meat and the shell near the tail.

Prick the meat using the fork.
Place on the serving plate.

SMOKED FISH

SMOKED SALMON

GUÉRIDON

1 pairs of service tongs
1 pair of fish bone tweezers
1 paring knife
1 hollow blade carving knife

1 plate for trimmings
Serving plates
1 smoked salmon
1 salmon board

PRESENTATION

Smoked salmon:
- a plate garnished with the first slices of salmon;
- two plates garnished with slices from the centre of the piece.

Loosen the skin from the bottom to the top of the salmon using the back of the spoon.

Cut the loosened skin using the paring knife.

Cut a thin slice to begin with, starting a quarter of the way up the piece, using the hollow blade carving knife.

Place it in the plate for trimmings.

Prick the skin to hold the piece of salmon.

Cut thin slices to the same length as the first slice.

Unfold the slice onto the plate using the knife.

Remove the fish bones with the tweezers as you cut slices.

Cut the skin along the back.

Cut and remove the ventral fin to continue cutting the slice.

Prick the skin to hold the salmon.

Cut thin slices to the same length as the first slice from the entire salmon.

Remove each slice by scraping the skin knife blade.

Unfold the slice onto the plate using the knife.

Remove the fatty part at the bottom of the slice using the paring knife (you can cut off the fat from the salmon before slicing).

Remove large visible fish bones with the tweezers before continuing to slice.

SMOKED EEL AND TROUT

GUÉRIDON

1 pair of tongs
1 hollow blade carving knife
1 paring knife
1 plate for trimmings

1 chopping board
Serving plates
1 smoked eel
1 smoked trout

PRESENTATION

Smoked eel and trout:

• three garnished plates;

• a dish with the remaining smoked eel and a smoked trout.

Cut the trout skin at the head, tail and along the stomach.

Hold the trout by gently pricking the bone behind the head inside the fish.

Slide the spoon between the flesh and skin to loosen them.

Completely remove the trout from the skin.

Place the trout on the serving plate.

Place the eel on the chopping board.

Cut the first slice off using the carving knife.

Cut sections eight to ten centimetres long.

Cut the skin on each side of the first section.

Remove the skin using the paring knife.

Roll the skin around the prongs of the fork to completely remove it.

Hold the first section by pricking it near the bone.

Slice it thinly, cutting flat against the bone.

Continue slicing each side of the bone.

Prick the second section in the middle, between the two fillets.

Cut along the bone.

Cut thin slices perpendicular to the bone.

Place on the serving plates.

FISH

GRILLED SALMON STEAK (A)
POACHED POLLOCK STEAK (B)

GUÉRIDON A

1 pair of tongs
1 warm serving plate
1 plate for trimmings
1 warm preparation plate
1 accumulation plate
1 grilled salmon steak

Can be presented on embossed paper.

GUÉRIDON B

1 pair of tongs
1 warm serving plate
1 plate for trimmings
1 warm preparation plate
1 accumulation plate
1 poached pollock steak

PRESENTATION

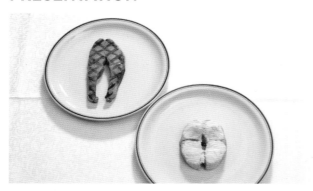

A grilled salmon steak and a poached pollock steak.

Slide the fork and spoon under the steak and place it on the preparation plate (stomach to the bottom of the plate).

Slide the prongs of the fork between the flesh and the skin at the stomach.

Hold the flesh with the spoon.

Roll the skin around the fork prongs.

If necessary, use the spoon to help you cut between the flesh and the skin.

Rotate the plate.

Continue to roll the skin.

Rotate the plate.

Finish rolling the skin and place it on the plate for trimmings.

Rotate the plate with the stomach facing downwards.

Prick the hole of the spine.

Remove the flesh of each side of the bone using the spoon.

Hold the flesh with the spoon.

Remove the bone and place it on the plate for trimmings.

Place the steak on the serving plate.

GRILLED SEA BREAM
(2 PEOPLE)

GUÉRIDON

1 pair of tongs
1 table knife
1 warm preparation plate

1 plate for trimmings
4 warm serving plates

PRESENTATION

Half of a grilled sea bream per plate.

PRESENTATION

A dorsal and ventral fillet per plate.

1st filleting method

Place the sea bream on the preparation plate with the head at the top and hold the back with the fork.

Cut the head with the blade of the spoon and place it in the plate for trimmings.

Hold the sea bream with the back of the fork.

Cut the skin along the stomach and backbone.

Hold the seam bream with the back of the fork at the tail fin. Lift the two upper fillets with the spoon and place them in the dish.

Hold the sea bream as before.

Slide the spoon between the central bone and lower fillets, remove the central bone and place it in the plate for trimmings.

Remove the dorsal fin barbs with the spoon and place them in the plate for trimmings.

Remove the ventral bones and place the lower fillets on the dish.

2nd filleting method

Cut around the head and along the central bone using the knife.

Remove two upper fillets one after the other and place them in the dish.

Rotate the plate with the head facing downwards.

Slide the spoon under the central bone to remove it with the head.

Serve the lower fillets on the plate and separate them.

SEA BREAM
(4 PEOPLE)

GUÉRIDON

1 pair of tongs
1 table knife
1 plate for trimmings

4 warm serving plates
1 accumulation plate
1 sea bream for 4 people

PRESENTATION

Sea bream for 4 people:

• one piece of the upper fillet and lower fillet per plate;

• one piece from the 'head' side and one from the 'tail' side per plate.

Hold the sea bream with the back of the fork.

Cut around the head, along the central bone and along the stomach using the knife.

Separate the two upper fillets using the knife and fork.

Slide the two upper fillets out on each side of the seam bream using the spoon and fork.

Rotate the dish and slide the spoon between the lower fillets and central bone.

Remove the bone and head and place them on the plate for trimmings.

Slide the blade of the spoon under the large ventral bones and remove them using a fork.

Remove the dorsal fin barbs with the back of the spoon and place them in the plate for trimmings.

Rotate the dish and separate each fillet into two parts.

Serve one piece of ventral fillet from the 'tail' side and one piece of the dorsal fillet from the 'head' side on each plate.

If the sea bream has been cooked in the oven, it may need to be skinned.

COLD SALMON

GUÉRIDON

1 pair of tongs
1 sole knife
1 plate for trimmings

20 serving plates
1 cold poached 3kg salmon

PRESENTATION

A buffet with ten plates for the slicing of a half salmon.

Cut the slices required in the direction of the salmon flesh using a sole knife.

Separate the ventral and dorsal sections in thin slices cut perpendicular to the central bone along the length of the salmon.

Finish cutting each section in the centre of the salmon.

Continue cutting sections starting at the ventral part of the salmon.

Slide the spoon under the central bone at the tail bone and remove it.

Break the bone in two and place the adjoining part of the tail bone in the plate for trimmings.

Slide the spoon under bone behind the head.
Break it up using the fork prongs.
Place the bone in the plate for trimmings.

SAUTÉED SOLE

GUÉRIDON A

1 pair of tongs
1 warm preparation plate
1 warm serving plate

1 plate for trimmings
1 accumulation plate
1 sautéed sole

PRESENTATION

Sautéed sole:
• sole meunière (top left and right);
• grilled sole (bottom left);
• fried sole (bottom right).

Place the sole in a preparation plate with the head at the top.

Push with the blade of the spoon behind the head.

Remove the head by lifting it with the spoon using a fork and place it in the plate for trimmings.

Hold the sole with the back of the fork.

Remove the barbs on each side of the sole.

Place barbs on the plate for trimmings.

Place the sole on the serving plate.

Cut along the bone with the blade of the spoon to separate the two upper fillets.

Separate the two upper fillets and slide them away from the bone.

Hold the sole with the back of the fork at the tail fin.

Scrape along the bone with the blade of the spoon in one motion from the head to the tail to remove it.

Slide the spoon between the bone and the upper fillets.

Move the spoon along until the tail fin.

Break the bone by pinching it between the spoon and fork.

Place the bone in the plate for trimmings.

This can be carried out without removing the head, which is removed in the last step.

GRILLED SOLE

GUÉRIDON

1 pair of tongs
1 warm preparation plate
1 plate for trimmings

3 warm serving plates
1 accumulation plate
3 grilled soles

PRESENTATION

Grilled sole.

Place the first sole in a preparation plate with the head at the top.

Push with the blade of the spoon behind the head.

Slide the fork under the head.

Remove the head by lifting it with the spoon and place it in the plate for trimmings.

Hold the sole with the back of the fork.

Remove the barbs on each side of the sole.and place them on the plate for trimmings.

Put the sole back in the dish to keep it warm.

Place the sole on the preparation plate.

Remove the head and the barbs.

Put the second sole back in the dish to keep it warm.

Place the third sole on the preparation plate.

Remove the head and the barbs; put the sole back in the dish.

Take the first sole, place it in the preparation plate and remove the upper fillets.

Remove the upper fillets and place them in the serving plate.

Remove the bone and place it on the plate for trimmings.

Separate the fillets and place them on the serving plate.

This can be carried out without removing the head, which is removed in the last step.

FRIED SOLE

GUÉRIDON

1 large spoon
2 forks
1 warm serving plate

1 plate for trimmings
1 warm preparation plate
1 fried sole

PRESENTATION

Fried sole.

Place the sole in a preparation plate with the head at the top.

Push with the blade of the spoon behind the head.

Remove the head by lifting it with the spoon using a fork and place it in the plate for trimmings.

Hold the sole with the back of the fork.

Cut along the central bone with the blade of the spoon.

Prick both forks on each side of the central bone.

Separate the fillets from the central bone.

Move the spoon along until the tail fin.

Break the bone by pinching it between the spoon and fork.

Place the bone in the plate for trimmings.

This can be carried out without removing the head, which is removed in the last step.

POACHED TROUT (A)
TRUITE AU BLEU (B)

GUÉRIDON A

1 pair of tongs
1 table knife
1 warm preparation plate
3 warm serving plates
1 plate for trimmings
1 accumulation plate
3 poached trout

PRESENTATION

Poached trout.

GUÉRIDON B

1 pair of tongs
1 table knife
1 warm preparation plate
2 warm serving plates
1 plate for trimmings
1 accumulation plate
2 truites au bleu

PRESENTATION

Truites au bleu.

Place the skinned trout back in the court bouillon.

Slide the fork behind the head and the spoon under the tail fin.

Place the trout on the preparation plate.

Hold the trout along the back with the spoon.

Slide the fork under the trout with the back of the fork against the skin. Turn over the trout.

Hold the trout with the back of the fork.

Cut the skin along the stomach from behind the head along the back to the tail fin.

Turn the plate so that the stomach is facing downwards and the head is turned to the right.

Slide the knife blade under the skin, starting at the head.

Remove the skin and place it on the plate for trimmings.

Hold the trout along the back with the spoon.

Slide the fork under the trout with the back of the fork against the skin.

Turn over the trout.

Slide the knife blade under the skin, starting at the head.

Remove the skin and place it on the plate for trimmings.

Turn the plate so that the stomach is facing downwards and the head is turned to the left.

Remove the gill cartilage using the tongs.

Place the trout on the serving plate.

The truite au bleu is normally cracked when presented as the trout is placed in the court bouillon alive.

POACHED TURBOT SECTION

GUÉRIDON

1 pair of tongs
1 warm preparation plate
1 plate for trimmings

2 warm serving plates
1 accumulation plate
2 turbot sections

PRESENTATION

Poached turbot sections.

Hold the turbot with the back of the fork.

Slide the end of the spoon between the black skin and the flesh.

Separate the flesh, leaving the skin stuck to the napkin.

Hold the turbot with the back of the fork at the barbs.

Slide the spoon between the flesh and white skin.

Remove the white skin and place it on the plate for trimmings.

Hold the turbot with the back of the fork at the barbs.

Slide the spoon between the upper fillet and bone.

Remove the fillet and place it on the serving plate.

Remove the barbs and place them on the warm serving plate.

Hold the bone with the back of the fork.

Slide the spoon between the bone and the lower fillets.

Remove the bone.

Place the lower fillet and barbs on the warm serving plate.

SMALL TURBOT

GUÉRIDON

1 pair of tongs
1 plate for trimmings
4 warm serving plates
1 accumulation plate
1 small turbot for 4 people

PRESENTATION

Small turbot fillets (half ventral fillet and half dorsal fillet served together per plate).

Hold the fish with the back of the fork.

Cut the skin and flesh around the head and along the central bone with the blade of the spoon.

Cut each side of the fish between the barbs and fillets.

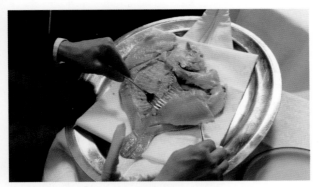

Slide the spoon and fork under the ventral fillets to remove them.

Place the fillets on the blade of the dish on either side of the head.

Rotate the dish and slide the spoon under the bone at the tail fin.

Hold the bone with the spoon and fork, break it and place it in the plate for trimmings.

Remove the rest of the bone.

Slide the spoon under the barbs and remove them.

Keep them on the blade of the plate.

Hold the flesh with the back of the fork.

Slide the fork under the lateral bones, remove them and place them in the plate for trimmings.

Split the ventral fillet into two using the blade of the spoon and serve the two parts on two plates.

Split the dorsal fillet opposite the ventral fillet into two and serve the two parts next to the other portions; garnish with the barbs.

Use the spoon to remove the cheek and flesh around the gills in the cartilage.

Turn the head and do the same for the other cheek.

POULTRY

DUCK
(4 PORTIONS)

GUÉRIDON

1 pair of tongs
1 table knife
1 sole knife
1 warm carving plate
1 plate for trimmings
1 accumulation plate
1 duck

PRESENTATION

Carved duck.

Place the blade of the knife in the neck opening.

Prick the tail end.

Drain the duck, place it on its side in the carving plate with the wishbone to the client and legs to the left.

Prick the thigh meat between the drumstick bone and thigh fat bone.

Cut the skin around the thigh.

Hold the duck under the wing with the flat edge of the knife blade.

Pull the thigh and remove it by cutting the joint ligaments.

Cut the rest of the leg in the plate for trimmings.

Cut and separate the drumstick from the thigh fat, serve the two pieces on the plate and rotate the duck.

Apply the same method to the other thigh.

Prick the duck in the sides, spike the spine to hold it in place with the tail at the top of the plate.

Cut the skin on either side of the wishbone and carve the first aiguillette.

Cut the aiguillettes from the wing to the wishbone.

Serve the aiguillettes on the serving dish using the knife.

Finish carving the aiguillettes.

Rotate the duck to have the tail facing yourself, prick it and carve the aiguillettes. Serve them on the serving dish.

Finish carving the aiguillettes.

Serve on the serving dish.

DUCK
(6 PORTIONS)

GUÉRIDON

1 pair of tongs
1 table knife
1 sole knife
1 warm board
1 plate for trimmings
1 accumulation plate
1 duck

PRESENTATION

Carved duck.

Place the blade of the knife in the neck opening.

Prick the tail end.

Drain the duck, place it on its side on the chopping board with the wishbone to the client and legs to the left.

Prick the thigh meat between the drumstick bone and thigh fat bone.

Cut the skin around the thigh.

Hold the duck under the wing with the flat edge of the knife blade.

Pull the thigh and remove it by cutting the joint ligaments.

Cut the rest of the leg in the plate for trimmings.

Sever the joint, cut the drumstick and serve the two pieces on the plate and rotate the duck.

Apply the same method to the other half.

Place the duck on its back again.

Prick the duck in the sides, spike the spine to hold it in place.

Hold the duck with the tail at the top of the serving dish.

Cut on either side of the wishbone using the sole knife.

Carve the first aiguillette.

Serve it on the serving dish using the knife.

Carve thin aiguillettes from the wing to the wishbone.

Serve the aiguillettes on the plate as you go.

Remove the wing using the paring knife.

Sever the joint.

Remove the fork and serve the wing on the serving dish.

Rotate the duck to have the tail facing the bottom, prick it in its sides again and carve the aiguillettes. Serve them on the serving dish as you go.

Rotate the duck, remove the wing and serve it on the serving dish.

TURKEY

GUÉRIDON

1 pair of tongs
1 sole knife
1 table knife
1 chopping board

1 plate for trimmings
Serving plates
1 turkey

PRESENTATION

Plates with aiguillettes and slices from the thigh and
rest of the turkey.

Place the turkey on the chopping board.

Remove the thighs.

Separate the drumstick from the fat.

Prick the thigh fat along the bone.

Cut thin slices parallel to the bone.

Prick drumstick along the bone.

Apply the same method to the thigh fat.

Serve the slices on the plates.

Prick the turkey in the sides and spike the spine to hold it in place (tail at the top of the plate).

Carve the first aiguillette.

Continue carving thin aiguillettes from the wing to the wishbone.

Serve the aiguillettes on the plates as you go using the knife.

The nerve drumstick is not always served.

PIGEON

GUÉRIDON

1 pair of tongs
1 table knife
1 warm carving plate

1 plate for trimmings
1 accumulation plate
2 pigeons

PRESENTATION

Carved pigeons.

Slide the fork and spoon under the pigeon wings.

Place the pigeon on the carving plate on its back with its legs to the left.

Prick the pigeon in its sides and push the prongs in along the spine.

Separate the pigeon breast in two following the wishbone.

Sever the sides along the spine on the opposite side to the fork prongs.

Carve the leg of the first half and serve it on the serving dish.

Sever the sides.

Remove the spine from the second half.

Carve the leg of the second half or just the wing.

SQUAB

GUÉRIDON

1 pair of tongs
1 table knife
1 warm carving plate
1 plate for trimmings

2 warm serving plates
1 accumulation plate
2 squabs

PRESENTATION

Carved squabs.

Slide the fork and spoon under the squab wings.

Place the squab on the carving plate on its back with its legs to the left.

Prick the spine above the tail inside the squab.

Sever the spine.

Rotate the squab to carve the other side.

Remove the two thighs.

Carve the legs, serve the two thighs, turning them over on the serving plate.

Prick the spine between the two wings.

Cut the sides each side of the fork and remove the rest of the spine.

Place the breast on the serving plate.

GRILLED CHICKEN

GUÉRIDON

1 pair of tongs
1 table knife
1 warm board

1 plate for trimmings
1 accumulation plate
1 grilled chicken

PRESENTATION

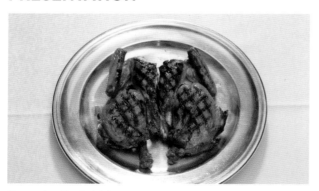

Carved grilled chicken.

Slide the fork and spoon under the chicken and place it on the chopping board with the legs to the left.

Prick the thigh meat between the drumstick bone and thigh fat bone.

Cut the skin around the thigh.

Remove the thigh.

Hold the right thigh on the plate for trimmings and cut the end of the leg.

Hold the thigh flat on the chopping board.

Sever the joint between the drumstick and thigh fat and serve the thigh on the serving dish.

Apply the same method to the other half.

Hold the breast along the wishbone using the fork.

Cut along the wishbone to remove the fillet.

Serve the fillet on the serving dish.

Hold the wishbone.

Cut along the wishbone to remove the other fillet.

Serve the fillet on the serving dish.

CHICKEN
(4 PORTIONS)

GUÉRIDON

1 pair of tongs
1 table knife
1 warm carving plate
1 plate for trimmings
1 accumulation plate
1 chicken

PRESENTATION

Carved chicken.

Alternative presentation:

Thigh fat or drumstick back towards the outside of the plate.

Place the blade of the knife in the neck opening.

Prick the spine above the tail.

Drain the chicken, place it on its side on the carving plate with the wishbone to the client and legs to the left.

Prick the thigh meat between the drumstick bone and thigh fat bone.

Cut the skin around the thigh.

Hold the chicken under the wing with the flat edge of the knife blade.

Pull the thigh and remove it by cutting the joint ligaments.

Hold the thigh upright on the plate for trimmings.

Carve the leg.

Hold the thigh on the carving plate, sever the joint between the drumstick and thigh fat and serve the thigh on the serving dish. Rotate the chicken. Apply the same method to the other thigh.

Prick the chicken in the sides, spike the spine to hold it in place.

Cut along the wishbone, loosen the fillet next to the fork.

Finish removing the fillet using the knife.

Sever the wing joint.

Apply the same method to the other fillet, without removing the fork.

Serve the fillets on the serving dish.

Hold the carcass with the fork prongs mounted on the wishbone.

Cut the meat at the tip of the wishbone.

Tip the wishbone.

Sever the joints on either side of the neck opening.

Serve the wishbone on the serving dish.

Place the carcass on its side.

Prick the carcass in the side.

Remove the oysters using the spoon and serve them on the serving dish.

The wishbone is not always served but the tail may be served.

CHICKEN
(5 PORTIONS)

GUÉRIDON

1 pair of tongs
1 table knife
1 warm carving plate
1 plate for trimmings
1 accumulation plate
1 chicken

PRESENTATION

Carved chicken.

Alternative presentation:
Thigh fat or drumstick back towards the outside of the plate.

Place the blade of the knife in the neck opening.

Prick the spine above the tail.

Drain the chicken, place it on its side on the carving plate with the wishbone to the client and legs to the left.

Prick the thigh meat between the drumstick bone and thigh fat.

Cut the skin around the thigh.

Hold the chicken under the wing with the flat edge of the knife blade.

Pull the thigh and remove it by cutting the joint ligaments.

Hold the thigh upright on the plate for trimmings.

Carve the leg.

Hold the thigh on the carving plate, sever the joint between the drumstick and thigh fat and serve the thigh on the serving dish, rotate the chicken.

Apply the same method to the other half.

Prick the chicken in the sides, spike the spine to hold it in place.

Carve the fillets leaving enough meat for the fifth portion and serve on the serving dish.

Lay the carcass down and prick it in the sides to hold it in place.

Loosen the meat on either side of the wishbone and sever the joints.

Rotate the carcass and prick through the sides.

Lift the carcass up to remove the meat, held using the knife.

Serve on the serving dish.

Hold the carcass upright on the plate.

Remove the oysters using a spoon.

Serve on the serving dish.

MEAT

RACK OF LAMB

GUÉRIDON

1 pair of tongs
1 table knife
1 warm board

Warm serving plates
1 accumulation plate
2 racks of lamb

PRESENTATION

Carved racks of lamb on plates and on a serving dish.

Prick the rack between the ribs, slide a spoon under the rack and place it upright on a board, with the meat facing the client.

Carve the ribs up to the fork.

Hold the rack with the back of the knife blade.

Remove the fork.

Prick the rack into the last rib.

Finish carving.

Serve the ribs on the serving dish crossed over each other.

3 ribs can be served by plate.

LEG OF LAMB

GUÉRIDON

1 pair of tongs
1 carving knife
1 boning knife
1 warm board
1 accumulation plate
1 leg of lamb
Have 1 cloth, 1 napkin or 1 muff ready to hold the leg

PRESENTATION

Sliced leg.

Hold the leg by the shaft using the napkin and place it on the chopping board with the cushion facing upwards.

Mark the knuckle around the bone using the carving knife.

Bone the knuckle and remove it.

Place the knuckle on the serving dish to keep it warm.

Turn the leg around and hold it with the stifle facing upwards.

Start thinly slicing the stifle carving flat towards the shaft.

Continue carving thin slices from the stifle, parallel to the bone.

Serve the slices on the serving dish using the knife, without pricking them.

Fully carve the stifle until you reach the bone.

Cut either side of the femur bone using the boning knife to make it easier to slice the cushion.

Turn the leg around and hold it with the cushion facing upwards.

Start on the cushion perpendicular to the bone.

Continue slicing slanting towards the femur bone.

Serve the slices as you go on the serving dish using the knife, without pricking them.

Gently cut either side of the bone to carve the last slices.

Place the knuckle on the serving dish and finely slice it.

Serve the portions on the serving dish.

SADDLE OF LAMB

GUÉRIDON

1 pair of tongs
1 carving knife
1 plate for trimmings

1 warm board
1 table stove and 1 dessert plate
1 saddle of lamb

PRESENTATION

4 served plates:
• left-hand plates with fillet, filet mignon and flap slices;
• right-hand plates with fillet and filet mignon slices.

The flap slices are not usually served to the client, they allow the saddle to remain pink.

Slide the fork and spoon under the saddle and place it on the chopping board.

Unroll the flaps.

Hold the saddle with the back of the fork.

Cut the first flap, turn the saddle and cut the second flap.

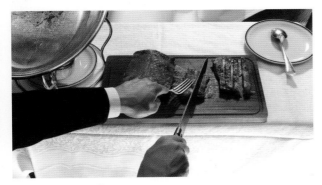

Finely slice the flaps.

Serve the strips on the serving dish crossed over each other.

Hold the saddle with the back of the fork.

Cut along the spine to the bone.

You may prick the spine to hold the saddle in place.

Hold the saddle with the back of the fork.

Slice the first fillet horizontally.

Serve the slices as you go, moving them to the serving dish on the flat edge of the knife.

Prick the saddle along the spine to hold it in place.

Apply the same method to the other side.

Turn the saddle and slice the first filet mignon.

Prick the fork into the 1st filet mignon.

Cut under the second filet mignon along the vertebrae.

Hold the saddle in place by pricking the spine.

Finely slice the second filet mignon and serve on the serving dish.

RIB OF BEEF
(2 PEOPLE)

GUÉRIDON

1 pair of tongs
1 slicing knife
1 chopping board
1 plate for trimmings

2 large warm serving plates
1 accumulation plate
1 rack of beef ribs

PRESENTATION

Carved beef ribs for two people.

Slide the spoon and fork under the beef ribs without pricking the meat.

Place the beef ribs on the chopping board.

Hold the beef ribs with the back of the fork to avoid pricking the meat.

Start removing the bone using the slicing knife.

Prick the membrane that covers the bone.

Fully remove the bone and place it on the plate for trimmings.

Hold the beef ribs with the back of the fork.

Remove the fat and place it on the plate for trimmings.

Hold the beef ribs with the back of the fork.

Start slicing at an angle, perpendicular to the bone.

Continue slicing to obtain 3 to 4 pieces per person.

Slide the flat edge of the knife under the reassembled beef ribs.

Hold the pieces at the tip of the knife with the fork.

Serve on the serving dish.

Serve alternate cuts on the plates to ensure the portions are even.

RIB STEAK
(2 PEOPLE)

GUÉRIDON

1 pair of tongs
1 table knife
1 warm carving plate
1 plate for trimmings

2 warm serving plates
1 accumulation plate
1 rib steak for 2 people

PRESENTATION

Rib steak served on two plates.

Slide the spoon and fork under the rib steak to move it.
Place the rib steak on the preparation plate.

Remove the fat around the cushion and place it on the plate for trimmings.

Hold the rib steak with the back of the fork.
At an angle, cut along the width to obtain 2 even portions.

You can cut at an angle to obtain 2 or 3 pieces per person.

Serve the portion where the slice appears on the plate.
Turn the other portion holding the rib steak between the spoon and back of the fork to present the slice.
Place on the serving plate.

PEPPERCORN STEAK

GUÉRIDON

1 pair of tongs, 2 dessert spoons,
1 dessert knife
10cl of crème fraîche
12cl of thick veal stock
20g butter
2cl Cognac
4 cl Porto
Salt

2 peppercorn steaks seared in the kitchen and brought
through in a very hot pan
1 table stove and 1 dessert plate
1 large warm flat plate
1 warm deep plate overturned to serve as a cloche
2 warm serving plates

PRESENTATION

Steaks coated in the sauce.

Turn on the table stove.

Remove the pan from the flame.

Pour Cognac into the side of the pan.

Put the pan back over the flame.

Place the edge of the pan over the flame.

Tilt the pan to light the alcohol vapours.

Remove the steaks, place them in the warm plate and cover them with the deep plate.

Deglaze with Porto.

Let the Porto reduce.

Add the veal stock.

Reduce a little.

Add crème fraîche.

Mix the sauce with the back of the fork.

Reduce a little until the sauce is thick enough to coat.

Reduce the table stove flame then add butter.

Hold the pan to the edge of the table stove.

Add lumps of butter and mix the sauce.

Add salt.

Place the steaks back in the pan and coat them in the sauce.

Let the steaks heat a little.

Turn off the table stove before serving the steaks.

STEAK TARTARE

GUÉRIDON

1 pair of tongs
1 deep plate
1 serving plate
1 plate for trimmings
Ketchup, Worcestershire sauce, Tabasco
Oil, mustard pot

Salt, pepper grinder
Beef mince
1 egg yolk
Chopped capers, onions and parsley
Paprika

PRESENTATION

Steak tartare.

Tip the egg yolk into the deep plate.

Add half a teaspoonful of mustard.

Pour the oil in gently.

Emulsify the yolk, mustard and oil.

Continue pouring oil in to obtain two large spoonfuls of mayonnaise.

Add the condiments and spices using the spoon.

Add 1 spoonful of ketchup, 1 dash of Worcestershire sauce and a few drops of Tabasco.

Mix to obtain a smooth tartare sauce.

Add the steak and mash it into the sauce.

Knead the steak and sauce using a spoon and fork until everything is well bound.

Place the lettuce leaf on the serving plate.

Form the steak and serve it on the plate.

Garnish the steak with onion rings (optional).

VEAL RIBS (A)
PORK RIBS (B)

GUÉRIDON A

1 pair of tongs
1 slicing knife
1 warm board
1 accumulation plate
1 rack of veal ribs

GUÉRIDON B

1 pair of tongs
1 slicing knife
1 warm board
1 accumulation plate
1 rack of pork ribs

PRESENTATION

Carved ribs:

• to the left: veal;

• to the right: pork.

Prick the rack between the ribs, slide a spoon under the rack and place it upright on a board, with the meat facing the client.

Cut off the first part.

Slice one rib along the bone and serve on the serving dish using a knife.

Slice the rib steak, ensuring you have an evenly thick slices.

Hold the rack with the back of the knife blade.

Remove the fork.

Serve the slice.

Prick the rack between the last two ribs.

Continue carving.

Cut the heel of the rib with the tip of the knife.

Continue to carving the ribs and rib steaks, serving them on the serving dish as you go.

Prick the last rib in the middle of the cushion, perpendicular to the meat fibres.

Slice the last rib.

Serve on the serving dish.

FLAMBÉED KIDNEY

GUÉRIDON

1 pair of tongs, 1 table knife,
2 dessert spoons, 1 dessert knife
10cl of crème fraîche
12cl of thick veal stock
20g butter
2cl Cognac, 4cl Porto
Salt
1 veal kidney cut in half, seared in the kitchen and
brought through in a very hot pan
1 table stove and 1 dessert plate
1 large warm flat plate
1 warm deep plate overturned to serve as a cloche
2 warm serving plates

PRESENTATION

Kidneys coated in the sauce.

Turn on the table stove.
Remove the pan from the flame.
Pour Cognac into the side of the pan.

Put the pan back over the flame.
Place the edge of the pan over the flame.
Tilt the pan to light the alcohol vapours.

Remove the kidney halves and place them on the warm plate.

Deglaze with Porto.

Let the Porto reduce.

Hold the kidney halves with the back of the fork and cut them along the lobes while keeping an eye on the reduction.

Cover the kidney pieces with the deep plate.

Add the veal stock.

Reduce a little.

Add crème fraîche.

Mix and reduce until the sauce is thick enough to coat.

Reduce the table stove flame then add butter.

Hold the pan to the edge of the table stove.

Add lumps of butter and mix the sauce.

Add salt.

Place the kidney pieces back in the sauce.

Coat the kidney pieces with the sauce.

Warm gently while stirring.

CHEESE WITH APPELLATION OF ORIGIN

SOFT CHEESE WITH A BLOOMY RIND

FABRICATION PROCESS

The curdle is poured by ladle into penetrated moulds, drained and then turned to be sprayed with mould spores (penicillium candidum) and salted on both sides. The cheese is then placed in the ripening room (controlled atmosphere) to allow the layer of mould to develop.

The cheese is ripened in a temperate cellar (12° C) for around ten days (to allow the cheese to transform evenly with the mould).

APPELLATION	PRESENTATION	MILK	PRODUCTION REGION	IN THE SAME FAMILY
BRIE DE MEAUX	Flat cylinder: - diameter: 42 to 54 cm - thickness: 2 to 3 cm	Cow	Île-de-France	
BRIE DE MELUN **(Natural rind)**	The same, but: - smaller - thicker: 4.5 cm	Cow	Île-de-France	
CAMEMBERT **DE NORMANDIE**	Flat round cheese (350-400g): - diameter: 11 cm - thickness: 2 to 3 cm	Cow	Normandy	- **Coulommiers** (Île-de-Fance) - **Cœur de Bray** (Normandy) - **Carré de l'Est** (Champagne) - **Pithiviers** (Orléannais)
CHAOURCE	Quite high cylinder: - diameter: 5 cm - thickness: 6 to 8 cm	Cow	Champagne	
NEUFCHÂTEL	Different shapes (from 100-300g): - cylinder - heart - square - brick	Cow	Normandy	

Cut a portion to size, stopping at a quarter of the diameter (half of the radius).

A dessert plate can be used to mark out a quarter of the diameter.

Continue cutting portions in the outer circle, leaving the inner cylinder intact.

Cut out a matching portion from the centre of the Brie.

Continue to cut portions from the inner part.

Cut a portion to size from the centre.

Cut a portion to size from the centre.

Cut a portion to size from the centre.

Cut a portion to size from the centre.

SOFT CHEESE WITH A WASHED RIND

FABRICATION PROCESS

Similar to the last group but cheeses with a washed rind:
• are usually thicker;
• are not sprayed with mould and are regularly washed with salted water (by hand, with a brush or with a sponge), in order to prevent mould from growing and encourage the development of 'red' bacteria, which give

the cheese their characteristics once mature (development of specific taste and flavours);
• have a much longer maturation period (3-4 months).

APPELLATION	PRESENTATION	MILK	PRODUCTION REGION	IN THE SAME FAMILY
LIVAROT (Colonel)	Flat cylinder: - diameter: 12 cm - thickness: different thicknesses	Cow	Normandy	
MAROILLES	Square shape (800g - 1kg): - sides from 10 to 20cm	Cow	Thiérache	**- La Boulette d'Avesnes** (Thiérache, Flanders) **- L'Époisse** (Burgundy) **- Le Rollot** (Picardy) **- Vacherin of Joux**
MUNSTER **OR MUNSTER GÉROMÉ**	Flat cylinder: - diameter: 10-30cm - thickness: 3 to 5 cm	Cow	Alsace	
PONT-L'ÉVÊQUE	Square shape: - sides from 10 to 20cm	Cow	Normandy	
MONT-D'OR **OR VACHERIN** **OF HAUT-DOUBS** **(to be eaten by spoon)**	Small round flat cheese: - diameter: 8 to 15 cm - thickness: 1.5 cm	Cow	Franche Comté (Massif du Mont-d'Or)	

Cut a portion to size from the centre.

Cut a portion to size from the centre.

Cut a portion to size from the centre.
Continue to cut portions as you would for round cheeses (Camembert).

Cut a rectangular portion to size from the side of the cheese.
Continue to cut towards the centre.
Follow the same process for each quarter.

Cut a portion to size from the centre.

Continue to cut portions as you would for round cheeses (camembert).

Cut a rectangular portion to size from the side of the cheese.

Continue to cut towards the centre.

Follow the same process for each quarter.

Cut a portion to size from the centre.

When fresh, this cheese is sometimes served with a spoon.

GOAT'S CHEESE

FABRICATION PROCESS

The fabrication process is similar to the one followed for soft cheeses with a bloomy rind. However, the moulds used vary in shape and the drying plays a greater role (affecting the hardness of the cheese). Some are dusted with wood charcoal ash.
Goat's cheeses are sold fresh, mature or very dry.

Note on the labelling:
• "pure goat's cheese": goat's milk only;
• "semi-goat's cheese": at least 50% goat's milk:
• "cheese with goat's milk": 25 to 49% goat's milk.

APPELLATION	PRESENTATION	MILK	PRODUCTION REGION	IN THE SAME FAMILY
CROTTIN DE CHAVIGNOL	Small round cheeses (70g)	Goat	Berry	- **Le Cabécou de Rocamadour** (Quercy) - **Le Sainte-Maure avec paille** (Touraine) - **Le Valençay** (Berry) - **Le Chabichou** (Poitou)
PICODON DE L'ARDECHE OU PICODON DE LA DRÔME (Dieu-le-Fit)	Small cylinder (150g)	Goat	Dauphiné	
POULIGNY-SAINT-PIERRE	Small, tall pyramid "Eiffel Tower shaped" (250g)	Goat	Berry	
SELLES-SUR-CHER	Small flat cone trunk (120-150g) "bluish"	Goat	Berry	

CROTTIN DE CHAVIGNOL

Cut a portion to size from the centre.
The Crottin can be cut directly into two portions.

PICODON DE L'ARDECHE

OU

PICODON DE LA DRÔME

Cut a portion to size from the centre.
The Picodon can be cut directly into two portions.

POULIGNY SAINT-PIERRE

Cut a portion to size from the centre.

SELLES-SUR-CHER

Cut a portion to size from the centre.

SAINTE-MAURE

Cut off the first part.
Remove the straw as you continue cutting portions.
Cut portions to size.

COLD-PRESSED CHEESE

FABRICATION PROCESS

The curdle is drained via the pressing process and then salted.

The maturation period takes 1-4 months. Some are washed to remove parasitic mould (Saint-Paulin) and others are also scraped to prevent the rind from getting too thick. The rind can be replaced by paraffin wax to better protect the cheese (Holland).

APPELLATION	PRESENTATION	MILK	PRODUCTION REGION	IN THE SAME FAMILY
CANTAL OR FOURME DU CANTAL	"Wheel" - large cylinder (25-50kg): - height: ±60 cm	Cow	Auvergne	
LAGUIOLE	"Wheel" - large cylinder (45kg): - height: ±60 cm	Cow	Auvergne	- **Murol** (Auvergne) - **Savaron** (Auvergne) - **Morbier** (France-Comté) - **Edam and Gouda** (Dutch) - **Tome de Savoie** (Savoie)
OSSAU-IRATY	"Tome"- cylinder (4 kg): - height: 10 to 12 cm	Ewe	Basque Country	
SAINT-NECTAIRE	Flat cylinder (± 2kg): - height: 3 to 4 cm	Cow	Auvergne	
SALERS	"Wheel"- cylinder (±50 kg): - height: 40 to 50 cm	Cow	Auvergne	
REBLOCHON	Round cheese (500g): - diameter: 14cm - height: 3 cm	Cow	Savoie	

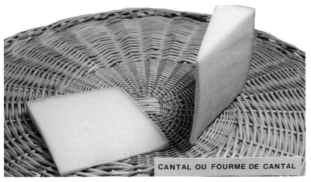

Cut a slice of around 2-3cm wide starting from the centre.

Cut portions to size perpendicular to the rind.

Cut a quarter of the wheel.

Cut a slice of around 2-3cm from the quarter.

Cut portions to size perpendicular to the rind.

Cut a slice of around 2-3cm.

Start by cutting portions parallel to the rind.

Continue by cutting slices perpendicular to the rind.

Cut a portion to size from the centre.

Cut a portion to size from the centre.

Cut a quarter of the wheel

Cut a slice of around 2-3cm from the quarter.

Start by cutting portions parallel to the rind.

When you reach the halfway point, cut portions perpendicular to the rind.

CHEESE WITH APPELLATION OF ORIGIN

PASTURIZED PRESSED CHEESE

FABRICATION PROCESS

These cheeses, which are generally very big, are often called "large cheeses".

The curdle is heated (50/60 °C) for half an hour (to select heat-resistant germs) and drained via the pressing process. Once salted, the cheese is matured for 6-10 months in temperatures specific to each variety. Gruyère is matured at a temperature that promotes fermentation germs that produce carbon dioxide (holes), which is not the case for the Beaufort cheese. They are brushed during the maturation period to remove any mould.

APPELLATION	PRESENTATION	MILK	PRODUCTION REGION	IN THE SAME FAMILY
BEAUFORT	Flat cylinder or wheel (20-70kg): - diameter: 80 cm - height: 10 cm	Cow	Savoie - Dauphiné	**- French Emmental** **- Gruyère** "from Brittany, Normandy or Charente/Charente-Maritime"
GRUYÈRE DE COMTÉ OR COMTÉ	Flat cylinder (35-55kg)	Cow	Franche Comté	

Cut a quarter of the wheel.

Cut a slice starting from the centre of the wheel.

Cut a slice of around 2-3cm.

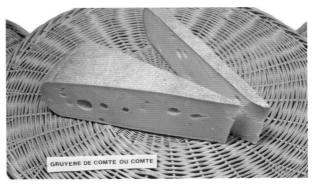

Cut a slice of around 2-3cm.

Cut the slice into two equal parts.

Cut portions to size parallel to the rind.

Cut the first slice into portions, parallel to the crust.
Cut the second slice perpendicular to the rind.
The portions may be trimmed, if necessary.

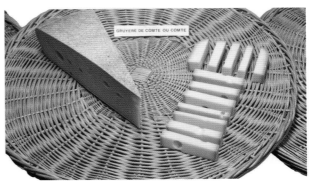

Finish by cutting slices perpendicular to the rind.

BLUE CHEESE

FABRICATION PROCESS

Blue cheeses are made following quite a similar process.

Moulds (penicillium glaucum, for example) are previously added to the curdle, which is then drained, placed into the mould and salted. The maturation period lasts several months, with the cheese being spiked (with needles) at the beginning to create air channels along which the aerobic mould (requiring air) will develop.

APPELLATION	PRESENTATION	MILK	PRODUCTION REGION	IN THE SAME FAMILY
BLEU D'AUVERGNE	Cylinder (4.5 kg): - diameter: 18 to 20 cm - height: 8 to 10 cm	Cow	Auvergne	
BLEU DES CAUSSES	Cylinder (4.5 kg): - diameter: 18 to 20 cm - height: 8 to 10 cm	Cow	Rouergue	

**BLEU DU HAUT-JURA
OR BLEU DE GEX
OR BLEU DE SEPTMONCEL**
	Cylinder (9 kg)	Ewe	Franche-Comté
			Gex
				- **Bleu de Bresse**
				- **Bleu de Saingorlon**
				  (mostly Auvergne)
				- **Bleu de Corse**
				  (ewe)

FOURME D'AMBERT OR DE MONTBRISON	Quite high cylinder: - diameter: 13 cm - height: 20 cm	Cow	Auvergne Livradois Forez	
ROQUEFORT	Cylinder: - Diameter: 20 cm - Height: 10 cm	Ewe	Rouergue Aveyron	

Cut into two equal parts.

Cut a slice of around 2-3cm wide starting from the centre.

Cut a portion to size starting from the centre of the slice.

Cut into two equal parts.

Cut a slice of around 2-3cm wide starting from the centre.

Cut a portion to size starting from the centre of the slice.

Cut into two equal parts.

Cut a slice of around 2-3cm wide starting from the centre.

Cut a portion to size starting from the centre of the slice.

Cut portions to size parallel to the rind.
Finish by cutting slices perpendicular to the rind.

Cut a quarter of the wheel.

Cut the cylinder into two equal parts.

Cut a slice of around 2-3cm thick from the quarter.

Cut a portion to size horizontally from the centre.

Start by cutting portions parallel to the rind.

A slice can be cut off the top of the half cylinder and then portions can be cut to size from the centre.

FRESH CHEESE

A-B: Demi-sel cheese cubes **C:** Rustic fromage frais **D:** "Faisselle" fromage frais **E:** Smooth fromage frais **F:** Cheese roll with fine herbs **G:** Little faisselle **H:** Low-fat fromage frais

FABRICATION PROCESS

The fresh curds are the first step in the fabrication process (they are never matured). The curd is simply placed into a mould and drained as required.

It is sold strained or smooth. Various ingredients may be added:
salt, crème fraîche, herbs...

MELTED CHEESE

A: Cocktail cubes. **B:** Crème Rambol. **C:** Hamburger cheese. **D:** Crème de Gruyère.

FABRICATION PROCESS

Melted cheeses are obtained by mixing melted hard cheeses, milk products (milk powder, cream or butter), emulsifiers, melting salts (lactic and citric acid, phosphates) and sometimes other ingredients (spices, herbs, ham...).

DESSERTS

FLAMBÉED BANANAS

GUÉRIDON

1 clamp
1 sugar sprinkler
20g butter
6cl rum

6 ½ bananas
2 warm serving plates
1 stove and 1 dessert plate
1 bi-metal pan or 1 heavy dish

PRESENTATION

Flambéed bananas.

Turn on the stove.

Melt 10g of butter.

Sprinkle sugar into the bottom of the pan.

Place the banana halves into the pan, flat side up.

Heat until the banana halves are golden, lower the stove temperature if necessary to avoid them burning.

Rotate the banana halves, starting with the one that was placed last, to avoid complication when turning them.

Allow the flat side to brown for a little while.

Sprinkle the banana halves with sugar.

Add a knob of butter, if necessary.

Leave to heat nicely.

Remove the pan from the flame.

Pour rum into the side of the pan.

Place the pan back over the flame, tilt the side over the stove flame to light the alcohol vapours, sprinkle with sugar while the bananas are flambéed.

Turn off the stove before serving the bananas.

BEURRE SUZETTE

GUÉRIDON

1 clamp, 1 table knife, 1 whisk
1 preparation plate
1 small salad bowl
200g butter softened in a large salad bowl

2cl Cognac, 2cl Grand Marnier
16 sugar cubes
1 sugar sprinkler
2 oranges, 1 lemon (well washed)

PRESENTATION

Beurre Suzette.

Sprinkle the butter with sugar (around four tablespoons).

Whisk the butter to blend it with the sugar.

Beat the butter and sugar mixture to obtain a pale creamy consistency.

Keep to one side.

Hold the orange on the plate and rub the angular edges of the sugar cubes on the zest (12 on the oranges, 4 on the lemon).

Place the sugar cubes in the small salad bowl.

Cut the oranges in half.

Squeeze the juice of the two oranges over the sugar cubes.

Crush the sugar cubes using a fork, to dissolve them in the orange juice.

Pour the sweet orange juice into the butter mixture.

Mix the orange juice and butter together using the whisk.

Pour in the Cognac and Grand Marnier.

Whisk briskly to obtain a smooth mixture.

FLAMBÉED CHERRIES

GUÉRIDON

1 clamp
1 sugar sprinkler
6cl Porto
4cl Kirsch

2 portions of drained Morello cherries
1 stove and 1 dessert plate
1 bi-metal pan or 1 heavy dish.

PRESENTATION

Flambéed cherries on ice cream
(brought in at the last minute).

Turn on the stove.

Pour the Porto into the pan.

Let the Porto reduce until you obtain a syrupy consistency.

Quickly add the drained cherries.

Sprinkle with caster sugar to absorb the juice that seeps out of the cherries.

Allow the juice to reduce.

Heat the pan.

Remove the pan from the flame.

Pour Kirsch into the side of the pan.

Place the pan back over the flame, tilt the side over the stove flame to light the alcohol vapours, sprinkle with sugar while the bananas are flambéed.

Turn off the stove before serving the cherries.

FLAMBÉED CRÊPES

GUÉRIDON

1 clamp
1 sugar sprinkler
1 lemon cut in two
8cl orange juice
2cl Grand Marnier
2cl Cognac
2 warm serving plates
6 crêpes
1 stove and 1 dessert plate
1 bi-metal pan or 1 heavy dish

PRESENTATION

Flambéed crêpes.

Turn on the stove.

Sprinkle caster sugar into the bottom of the pan.

Squeeze a lemon half over all of the pan by pricking the pulp with the fork and rotating it.

Leave the lemon and sugar to cook until a brown caramel is obtained.

Quickly pour the orange juice in all over the caramel.

Reduce the stove flame if necessary to avoid the mixture reducing too quickly.

Pick up a crêpe using the spoon and back of the fork.

Lay one side of the crêpe down in the sauce.

Turn it over to coat the other side in the sauce.

Fold the crêpe in two.

Fold the crêpe again into a quarter and place it to one side of the pan to allow you to prepare the other crêpes.

Once all of the crêpes are ready, heat the entire pan.

Remove the pan from the flame.

Pour Grand Marnier into the side of the pan.

Remove the pan from the flame.

Pour the Cognac in at the same place.

Place the pan back over the flame, tilt the side over the stove flame to light the alcohol vapours, sprinkle with sugar while the crêpes are flambéed.

Turn off the stove before serving the crêpes.

CRÊPES SUZETTE

GUÉRIDON

1 clamp
2 warm serving plates
Beurre Suzette

6 crêpes
1 stove and 1 dessert plate
1 bi-metal pan or 1 heavy dish

PRESENTATION

Crêpes Suzette.

Put half a spoonful of the butter into the pan.
Let it melt.

Pick up a crêpe using the spoon and back of the fork.
Lay one side of the crêpe down in the butter.

Turn it over to coat the other side in the butter. Fold the crêpe in two.

Fold the crêpe into a quarter and place to one side of the pan.
Prepare and fold another crêpe.

Add half a spoonful of butter.

Coat the other crêpes in the butter and fold them.
Place the crêpes to the sides of the pan and allow to brown a little.
Turn off the stove before serving the crêpes.

The crêpes can be flambéed for "crêpes Suzette flambées".

FLAMBÉED PEACHES

GUÉRIDON

1 clamp
1 sugar sprinkler
1 lemon cut in two
4cl Cointreau

4 peach halves in syrup
1 stove and 1 dessert plate
1 bi-metal pan or 1 heavy dish

PRESENTATION

Flambéed peaches on ice cream
(brought in at the last minute).

Turn on the stove.

Sprinkle caster sugar into the bottom of the pan.

Squeeze a lemon half over all of the pan by pricking the pulp with the fork and rotating it.

Leave the lemon and sugar to cook until a caramel is obtained.

Place the peach halves in the caramel, kernel side down, and prick them all over to allow the sauce to penetrate.

Add one or two spoonfuls of syrup, allow to brown.

Turn the peach halves over.

Heat well without burning.

Remove the pan from the flame.

Pour Cointreau into the side of the pan.

Place the pan back over the flame, tilt the side over the stove flame to light the alcohol vapours, sprinkle with sugar while the bananas are flambéed.

Turn off the stove before serving the peaches.

FRUIT

PINEAPPLE

GUÉRIDON

1 pair of tongs
1 serrated knife
1 paring knife
1 chopping board

1 serving dish
1 plate for trimmings
1 pineapple

PRESENTATION

Sliced pineapple.

Hold the pineapple by the leaves side down on the plate.

Cut off the base of the pineapple using a serrated knife.

Place the pineapple upright on the plate, holding it by the leaves.

Peel from top to bottom using a serrated knife.

Hold the pineapple on the board by the leaves.

Remove the black parts following the lines down the pineapple from top to bottom and place them on the plate for trimmings.

Cut 2-3cms deep around the core of the pineapple using the tip of the paring knife.

Start cutting thin slices using the serrated knife.

Using the paring knife, keep cutting into the core as you cut slices.

Slice the entire pineapple.

Remove the pre-cut core of the pineapple and serve the sliced on the plate using the pair of tongs.

PINEAPPLE (SOLD À LA CARTE)

GUÉRIDON

1 pair of tongs
1 serrated knife
1 paring knife
1 preparation plate

1 serving plate
1 plate for trimmings
1 pineapple

PRESENTATION

A portion of pineapple served on a plate and the rest of the pineapple.

Hold the pineapple by the base on the plate for trimmings.

Gently cut the pineapple below the leaves.

Keep the leafy part for presentation on the plate.

Peel the pineapple using the serrated knife to size for the number of slices required.

Hold the pineapple side down on the preparation plate.

Cut the number of slices desired.

Keep the rest of the pineapple for presentation on the plate.

Prick the core of the slice with the fork.

Remove the black parts around the edge and place them on the plate for trimmings.

Cut around the fork using the tip of the knife.

Remove the core.

Place the pineapple slice on the serving plate.

A cutter may be used to remove the core.

STRAWBERRIES

GUÉRIDON

1 pair of tongs
1 napkin on a plate
1 plate for trimmings

1 salad bowl filled with fresh water
2 serving plates
Strawberries

PRESENTATION

Strawberries.

Put a portion of strawberries in the fresh water to wash them.

Place the strawberries on the napkin to dry them.

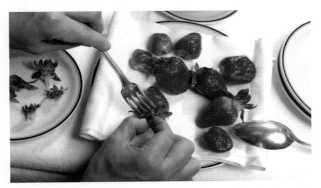

Hold the stalk and slide the fork between the flesh and the sepals.

Pull the stalk to remove the sepals and place them on the plate for trimmings.

Place the strawberries on the serving plate.

Put the second portion of strawberries in the water.
Place the strawberries on the napkin.
Remove the stalks.

Place the strawberries on the second serving plate.

EXOTIC FRUIT

GUÉRIDON

1 pair of tongs
1 paring knife
1 dessert fork
1 preparation plate

1 plate for trimmings
Serving plates
Mangoes, prickly pears, kiwis

PRESENTATION

Exotic fruit.

Slit the kiwi around the stalk, prick it vertically between the stalk and the incision using the dessert fork, cut a cap out from the opposite end.

Peel the kiwi along its length.

Cut the kiwi into thin slices on the serving plate.

Slit the prickly pear skin at the opposite end to the stalk, prick it at the incision, cut a cap out from the stalk end.

Peel the prickly pear along its length.

Cut the prickly pear into slices on the serving plate.

Slit the mango's skin around the stalk, prick it near the stalk, push the fork prongs towards the flat side of the stone, cut off the cap at the other end of the mango and remove the skin along its length.

Cut into the flesh from one side to the other of the stone and around it.

Cut half slices onto the preparation plate.

Place the half slices on the serving plate.

ORANGE

GUÉRIDON

1 pair of tongs
1 paring knife
1 preparation plate
1 plate for trimmings

2 serving plates
1 coupe on a plate
3 oranges

PRESENTATION

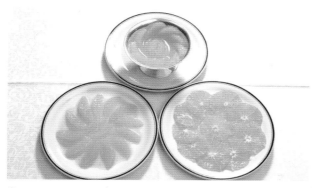

Orange supremes in a coupe and on a plate, and the slices on a plate.

1st slicing method

Remove the stem.

Cut into the skin around the stem.

Cut a cap off the opposite end to the stem.

Prick through the cap with the fork.

Hold the orange on the plate.

Prick the orange.

Peel the orange quickly.

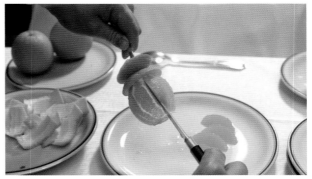

Cut out the supremes between the membrane, above the preparation plate in order to salvage the juice.

Serve the supremes in the coupe.

2nd slicing method

Peel the orange quickly.

Remove the fork holding the orange flat with the knife blade.

Prick the orange again, vertically near the incision.

Cut thin slices on the serving plate, remove the pips and core.

PEACH

GUÉRIDON

1 pair of tongs
1 paring knife
1 preparation plate

2 serving plates
1 plate for trimmings
2 peaches

PRESENTATION

One whole peach and peach sections.

Remove the stem.

Hold the peach on the plate to cut a thin cap off the opposite end to the stem.

Place the cap in the plate for trimmings.

Rotate the peach.

Cut a small base of the stem side and place it in the plate for trimmings.

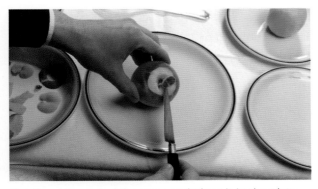

Cut the skin around the stem and place it in the plate for trimmings.

Prick the peach at the stem end and push the prongs of the fork in until they reach the stone of the peach.

Peel the peach and place the skin in the plate for trimmings.

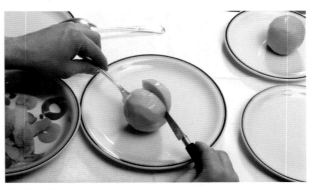

Cut the first section.

Continue to cut sections.

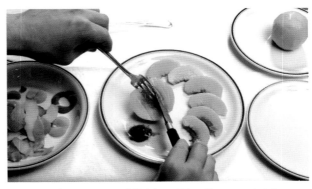

Remove the stone and finish cutting the peach into sections.

Place the sections on the serving plate.

APPLE - PEAR

GUÉRIDON

1 pair of tongs
1 paring knife
1 preparation plate

1 plate for trimmings
2 serving plates
1 apple and 1 pear

PRESENTATION

A whole apple and pear and apple sections (example of an apple broken while being prepared).

Remove the black part at the base of the fruit using the tip of the knife.

Cut a cone around the stem, keeping it for presentation.

Cut the bottom of the apple to create base.

Place removed parts on the plate for trimmings.

Hold the apple on its base.

Push the fork in vertically.

1st method

Peel the apple from the base towards the fork.

Place peelings on the plate for trimmings.

2nd method

Peel the apple in a spiral starting around the stem.

Hold the apple on its base.

Cut the apple in two slicing the knife blade between the fork prongs, separating the two halves.

Prick the core of the apple with the fork.

Cut a cone around the fork prongs.

Remove the cone and place it on the plate for trimmings.

Serve the apple on the plate, replace the stem and apply the same method to the pear.

PRESENTATION & PREPARATION OF CIGARS

PRESENTATION & PREPARATION OF CIGARS

CIGAR BOX

Designed to store cigars in optimal conditions, a cigar box automatically regulates and maintains the conditions inside at a humidity of 70 to 72% and a temperature between 16 to 18°C, irrespective of where the box is kept.

EQUIPMENT TO LIGHT A CIGAR

- Ash tray
- Candle holder (1 candle)
- Box of matches (long)
- Cigar
- Cigar cutter: for all cigar sizes, this allows you to make a clean cut for perfect smoking.

LIGHTING A CIGAR

Cut the cap off using the cigar cutter.

Leave the band around the cigar to avoid ripping its wrapper.

Concept

To light a cigar, a short and lively flame is needed, without odour (avoid lighters or wicks, for example).

After having lit the candle, take the cigar in your right hand.

Light a match with your left hand using the candle.

Light the cigar.

Keep the match flame around a centimetre below the foot of the cigar, which should be turned regularly between your fingers until the filler lights and ash begins to form.

SERVING METHODS FOR DIFFERENT DISHES

SOUPS

DISH	DISH DESCRIPTION WHEN SERVING
CONSOMMÉ BRUNOISE	• Clarified beef broth (pot-au-feu stock) garnished with diced vegetables (carrots, turnips, green beans) and peas.
CONSOMMÉ MADRILÈNE WITH CHEESE STRAWS	• Clarified beef broth (pot-au-feu stock) flavoured with celery and tomato (cheese straws: little puff pastry gruyère sticks)
POTAGE CULTIVATEUR	• Soup made from chopped vegetables sweated in butter with pork belly. • Served with thin bread slices dried in the oven and grated gruyère.
POTAGE JULIENNE DARBLAY	• Cream soup made from potato purée and leek whites (Parmentier), garnished with thin strips of sweated carrots, turnips, celery and leek whites.
POTAGE SAINT-GERMAIN WITH CROUTONS	• Soup made from crushed pea purée. • Served with white bread croutons fried in clarified butter.
POTAGE AMBASSADEUR	• Soup made from crushed pea purée (Saint-Germain), garnished with sorrel, lettuce and creole rice chiffonnade.
VELOUTÉ DUBARRY	• Soup made from cauliflower with crème fraîche and egg yolks, garnished with little cauliflower florets.
VELOUTÉ CHOISY	• Soup made from lettuce with crème fraîche and egg yolks. • Served with fried croutons.
ONION GRATIN	• Soup made from sliced thinly onions browned in butter thinned with beef consommé. • Onion soup may be served with a gratin of sliced bread and gruyère.
FISH SOUP	• Soup made from rockfish (red mullet, scorpion fish, weevers, conger...) with garnish of vegetables, aromatic plants and spices (onions, leeks, tomatoes, garlic, fennel, saffron...). • Served with garlic baguette slices, grated gruyère and an aïoli or rouille sauce.

COLD STARTERS

DISH	DISH DESCRIPTION WHEN SERVING
RAW VEGETABLES	• Assortment of chopped vegetables served raw with a sauce.
GREEK-STYLE VEGETABLES	• Vegetables (button mushrooms, artichokes, large and small onions, cauliflower, courgettes...) cooked with white wine, lemon juice, olive oil, pepper grains and coriander.
MIXED VEGETABLES WITH MAYONNAISE	• Assortment of little cubed vegetables (carrots, turnips, green beans) and peas with mayonnaise, garnished with boiled egg quarters and tomatoes.
AVOCADO AND PRAWNS	• Half avocado filled with prawns in cocktail sauce (mayonnaise, ketchup, tabasco, Worcestershire sauce, cognac).
SALADE NIÇOISE	• Salad with potatoes, tomatoes, green beans, peppers, tuna and lettuce, garnished with boiled eggs, black olives and anchovies, dressed with an olive oil vinaigrette.

| --- | --- | --- |
Warm consommé cup Saucer Dessert plate	Dessert spoon	Guéridon (table stove) If the cups are garnished in the kitchen: serve on a platter
Warm consommé cup Saucer Dessert plate Dessert Pair of tongs	Dessert spoon	Guéridon (table stove) If the cups are garnished in the kitchen: serve on a platter Garnish: English style
Large set-up plate Warm deep plate Ladle Dessert Pair of tongs (garnish)	Large spoon	Guéridon (table stove) Garnish: English style
Large set-up plate Warm deep plate Ladle Dessert Pair of tongs (garnish)	Large spoon	Guéridon (table stove)
Large set-up plate Warm deep plate Ladle Dessert Pair of tongs (garnish)	Large spoon	Guéridon (table stove) Garnish: English style
Large set-up plate Warm deep plate Ladle Dessert Pair of tongs (garnish)	Large spoon	Guéridon (table stove)
Large set-up plate Warm deep plate Ladle Dessert Pair of tongs (garnish)	Large spoon	Guéridon (accumulation plate)
Large set-up plate Warm deep plate Ladle Dessert Pair of tongs (garnish)	Large spoon	Guéridon (accumulation plate) Garnish: English style
Large set-up plate Dessert plate Bowl for grilling	Large spoon	On a platter (prepared in the kitchen or the serving bench)
Large set-up plate Warm deep plate Ladle Dessert Pair of tongs (garnish) Dessert spoon (sauce)	Large spoon	Guéridon (table stove) Garnish: English style

Large set-up plate Pair of tongs (based on the quantity of vegetables)	Large knife Large fork	Guéridon
Large set-up plate Large spoons (based on the quantity of vegetables)	Large knife Large fork	Guéridon
Large set-up plate Pair of tongs	Large knife Large fork	English
Dessert plate Pair of tongs	Dessert spoon	English or plate service
Large set-up plate Pair of tongs	Large knife Large fork	Guéridon

WARM STARTERS

DISH	DISH DESCRIPTION WHEN SERVING
ASPARAGUS WITH MOUSSELINE SAUCE	• Asparagus. • Mousseline sauce: hollandaise sauce with crème fraîche.
QUICHE LORRAINE	• Shortcrust pastry base garnished with lardons, gruyère and topped with a milk, cream and egg filling, seasoned with cayenne pepper and nutmeg.
ONION TART	• Shortcrust pastry base garnished with lardons and onions (white), topped with a milk, cream and egg filling, seasoned with cayenne pepper and nutmeg.
CHEESE STICKS	• Pastry sticks garnished with a béchamel and gruyère topping, seasoned with cayenne pepper and nutmeg.
ANCHOVY STICKS	• Pastry topped with anchovy butter.
TRIANGULAR TALMOUSES	• Triangular pastries garnished with a béchamel and gruyère topping, seasoned with cayenne pepper and nutmeg.
TALMOUSES À LA BAGRATION	• Shortcrust and choux pastry garnished with a béchamel and gruyère topping.
LITTLE PUFF PASTRIES	• Puff pastries garnished with sausage and cushion of veal, seasoned with cognac and Madeira wine, shallots, chervil and tarragon.
SAUCISSON IN BRIOCHE WITH A PORT SAUCE	• Poaching saucisson or Morteau sausage wrapped in brioche pastry, served with a port sauce.
CHEESE SOUFFLÉS	• Batter made from béchamel sauce, egg yolks, gruyère and whisked egg whites, served in a "soufflé" mould and cooked in the oven.

PASTA AND FLOUR-BASED DISHES

DISH	DISH DESCRIPTION WHEN SERVING
SPAGHETTI NAPOLITAN	• Spaghetti coated in butter, served with a tomato sauce, cooked tomatoes and parmesan or grated gruyère.
SPAGHETTI BOLOGNESE	• Spaghetti coated in butter, served with a bolognese sauce (minced beef tenderloin tail, onions and brown tomato veal stock), cooked tomatoes, parmesan or grated gruyère.
PARISIAN GNOCCHI	• Poached choux pastry baked and grilled in the oven topped with béchamel sauce and grated gruyère.
ROMAN-STYLE GNOCCHI	• Wheat semolina cooked with milk, butter, eggs and gruyère, shaped into different shapes and grilled.

EGGS

DISH	DISH DESCRIPTION WHEN SERVING
SOFT COOKED EGGS FLORENTINE	• Soft cooked eggs (liquid yolk) served on a bed of spinach and coated in Mornay sauce (béchamel with egg yolks and gruyère) then grilled.
CHIMAY FILLED EGGS	• Boiled egg halves scooped out and filled with a mixture of the yolks and a duxelle (mushroom purée with shallots and chopped parsley), coated in Mornay sauce and grilled.

SERVICE EQUIPMENT	EQUIPMENT USED TO SERVE	RECOMMENDED SERVICE STYLE
Large warm plate Pair of tongs (or 2 forks)	Large knife Large fork	Guéridon
Large warm plate Pair of tongs Large knife (slicing)	Large knife Large fork	Guéridon
Large warm plate Pair of tongs Large knife (slicing)	Large knife Large fork	Guéridon
Large warm plate Pair of tongs	Large knife Large fork	English
Large warm plate Pair of tongs	Large knife Large fork	English
Large warm plate Pair of tongs	Large knife Large fork	English
Large warm plate Pair of tongs Large knife (slicing)	Large knife Large fork	Guéridon
Large warm plate Pair of tongs Large knife (slicing)	Large knife Large fork	Guéridon
Large warm plate Pair of tongs Bread knife (slicing) Warm board Dessert spoon (sauce)	Large knife Large fork	Guéridon Sauce: English style
Large warm plate Pair of tongs	Large knife Large fork	Guéridon

SERVICE EQUIPMENT	EQUIPMENT USED TO SERVE	RECOMMENDED SERVICE STYLE
Large set-up plate Warm deep plate Pair of tongs Dessert spoon for the accompaniments	Large knife Large fork Large spoon	Guéridon (table stove)
Large set-up plate Warm deep plate Pair of tongs Dessert spoon for the accompaniments	Large knife Large fork Large spoon	Guéridon (table stove)
Large warm plate Pair of tongs	Large knife Large fork	Guéridon (accumulation plate)
Large warm plate Pair of tongs	Large knife Large fork	Guéridon (accumulation plate)

SERVICE EQUIPMENT	EQUIPMENT USED TO SERVE	RECOMMENDED SERVICE STYLE
Large warm plate Pair of tongs	Large knife Large fork	Guéridon (accumulation plate)
Large warm plate Pair of tongs	Large knife Large fork	Guéridon (accumulation plate)

DISH	DISH DESCRIPTION WHEN SERVING
COCOTTE EGGS WITH CREAM	• Soft-cooked eggs coated in reduced crème fraîche in a cassolette.
FRIED EGGS WITH POULTRY LIVERS	• Fried eggs garnished with a bunch of sautéed poultry livers and a drizzle of Madeira wine sauce.
JELLY AND HAM EGGS	• Poached eggs with cooked ham in jelly.
FRIED EGGS AND BACON	• Pan-fried eggs served with fried breadcrumbs, topped with grilled bacon slices and garnished with fried parsley.
PORTUGUESE SCRAMBLED EGGS	• Creamy whisked cooked eggs, to which cooked tomatoes are added.
OMELETTE WITH FINE HERBS	• Rolled omelette garnished with fine, freshly chopped herbs (parsley, chervil, tarragon, chives).
FLAT SPANISH-STYLE OMELETTE	• Flat omelette garnished with cooked tomatoes, onions, peppers and chopped parsley.

FISH

DISH	DISH DESCRIPTION WHEN SERVING
POACHED POLLOCK STEAK WITH MOUSSELINE SAUCE BOILED POTATOES	• Thick pollock steak poached in water, lemon and salt. • Mousseline sauce: hollandaise sauce with whipped cream. • Potatoes boiled in water.
POACHED HAKE STEAK WHITE BUTTER SAUCE BOILED POTATOES	• Hake steak poached in water, lemon and salt. • Butter emulsion made from a shallot, white wine and white wine vinegar reduction. • Potatoes boiled in water.
POACHED TURBOT SECTION HOLLANDAISE SAUCE BOILED POTATOES	• Thick turbot steak poached in water and milk. • Hollandaise sauce: warm emulsion made from egg yolks, butter and lemon. • Potatoes boiled in water.
TRUITE AU BLEU WHITE BUTTER SAUCE STEAMED POTATOES	• Live trout covered and coated in vinegar, poached in a boiling court bouillon. • Butter emulsion made from a shallot, white wine and white wine vinegar reduction. • Steamed potatoes
TROUT POACHED IN COURT BOUILLON MELTED BUTTER STEAMED POTATOES	• Trout poached in court bouillon. • Butter emulsion with lemon juice. • Steamed potatoes
ENGLISH-STYLE WHITING HERB BUTTER	• English-style boned and breaded whiting (coated in flour, beaten eggs and breadcrumbs), sautéed. • Softened butter with chopped parsley and lemon juice.
SOLE MEUNIÈRE BOILED POTATOES	• Sole cooked in a pan, sprinkled with lemon and brown frothy butter. • Potatoes boiled in water.
SOLE GRENOBLOISE BOILED POTATOES	• Meunière sole garnished with capers, lemon cubes and fried bread crumbs. • Potatoes boiled in water.

SERVICE EQUIPMENT	EQUIPMENT USED TO SERVE	RECOMMENDED SERVICE STYLE
Dessert plate (paper optional) Pair of tongs (or 2 forks)	Dessert spoon	English
Dessert plate Individual egg dishes	Dessert knife Dessert fork "dessert spoon"	Plate service (or platter)
Dessert plate Pair of tongs	Dessert knife Dessert fork "dessert spoon"	Guéridon
Warm dessert plate Pair of tongs	Dessert knife Dessert fork "dessert spoon"	Guéridon
Warm dessert plate Pair of tongs	Dessert fork Dessert spoon	English
Large warm plate Pair of tongs	Large knife Large fork	Guéridon (accumulation plate)
Large warm plate	Large knife Large fork	Plate service (or platter)

Large warm plate Pair of tongs Dessert spoon (sauce) Large spoon (potatoes)	Fish fork and knife	Guéridon Sauce: English style
Large warm plate Pair of tongs Dessert spoon (sauce) Large spoon (potatoes)	Fish fork and knife	Guéridon Sauce: English style
Large warm plate Pair of tongs Dessert spoon (sauce) Large spoon (potatoes)	Fish fork and knife	Guéridon Sauce: English style
Large warm plate Pair of tongs Fish spoon (cutting) Dessert spoon (sauce) Large spoon (potatoes)	Fish fork and knife	Guéridon Sauce: English style
Large warm plate Pair of tongs Fish spoon (cutting) Dessert spoon (sauce) Large spoon (potatoes)	Fish fork and knife	Guéridon (accumulation plate) Sauce: English style
Large warm plate Pair of tongs Two dessert spoons (herb butter in a sauce boat)	Fish fork and knife	Guéridon (accumulation plate) Butter (guéridon)
Large warm plate Pair of tongs Large spoon (potatoes)	Fish fork and knife	Guéridon (accumulation plate)
Large warm plate Pair of tongs Large spoon (potatoes)	Fish fork and knife	Guéridon (accumulation plate)

DISH	DISH DESCRIPTION WHEN SERVING
MEUNIÈRE TROUT BOILED POTATOES	• Trout cooked in a pan, sprinkled with lemon and brown frothy butter. • Potatoes boiled in water.
TRUITE GRENOBLOISE BOILED POTATOES	• Meunière trout garnished with capers, lemon cubes and fried bread crumbs. • Potatoes boiled in water.
GRILLED SOLE ANCHOVY BUTTER BOILED POTATOES	• Grilled sole (gridded surface) served with softened anchovy butter. • Potatoes boiled in water.
FRIED WHITING WITH LEMON	• Whiting coated in beer or salted milk then flour and fried (in oil). • Garnished with fried parsley and lemon.
MERLAN EN COLÈRE TARTARE SAUCE	• Fried whiting presented in a circle with its tail between its teeth. • Mayonnaise sauce with capers, gherkins and fine herbs.
SOLE COLBERT	• Boned sole, breaded English style and fried, garnished with lemon and fried parsley. • Herb butter.
SOLE BONNE FEMME	• Sole fillet poached in fish stock with white wine, on a bed of shallots, parsley and mushrooms. • Sauce made from the cooked reduction with cream and whisked with butter.
SOLE DIEPPOISE	• Fillet of sole poached in fish stock and white wine. • Sauce made from the cooked reduction with cream and whisked with butter. • Garnish made from prawns, muscles and our mushrooms.
SOLE MARGUERY	• Same preparation as for sole dieppoise but the sauce is ice cold (coloured in the salamander). • Florets: little puff pastry croissants.
BARBUE DUGLÉRÉ	• Brill fillet poached in fish stock with white wine, shallots, onion, parsley and tomatoes. • Sauce made from the cooked reduction whisked with butter.
AMERICAN-STYLE BURBOT PILAU RICE	• Fish fillet in a white wine, crustacean shell and tomato sauce. • Rice cooked in the oven with onions, butter and a bouquet garni.
SOLE NORMANDE	• Full poached sole coated in a white wine sauce, garnished with prawns, oysters, muscles, gudgeons (or smelt), crayfish, truffle slices, and "little puff pastry croissants".
RIESLING TROUT	• Trout poached in fish stock with Riesling (white wine from Alsace); the sauce is reduced, cream is added and it is whisked with butter. • Garnished with mushrooms, truffles and puff pastry croissants.

SHELLFISH

NANTAISE COQUILLES SAINT-JACQUES	• The roe and muscle of the scallop are cooked in white wine, cream is added and the sauce is whisked with butter. They are then garnished with prawns and muscles and presented in their shells.
MOULES MARINIÈRE	• Farmed muscles in white wine, butter, shallots and parsley (in their shells)
STUFFED MUSCLES	• Spanish muscles in their half shells garnished with garlic butter (butter, parsley, garlic, shallots) and breadcrumbs then grilled.

SERVICE EQUIPMENT	EQUIPMENT USED TO SERVE	RECOMMENDED SERVICE STYLE
Large warm plate Pair of tongs Large spoon (potatoes)	Fish fork and knife	Guéridon (accumulation plate)
Large warm plate Pair of tongs Large spoon (potatoes)	Fish fork and knife	Guéridon (accumulation plate)
Large warm plate Pair of tongs Large spoon (potatoes)	Fish fork and knife	Guéridon (accumulation plate)
Large warm plate Pair of tongs	Fish fork and knife	Guéridon
Large warm plate Pair of tongs Dessert spoon (sauce)	Fish fork and knife	Guéridon Sauce: English style
Large warm plate Pair of tongs	Fish fork and knife	Guéridon
Large warm plate Pair of tongs	Fish fork and knife	Guéridon (accumulation plate)
Large warm plate Pair of tongs	Fish fork and knife	Guéridon (accumulation plate)
Large warm plate Pair of tongs	Fish fork and knife	Guéridon (accumulation plate)
Large warm plate Pair of tongs	Fish fork and knife	Guéridon (accumulation plate)
Large warm plate Pair of tongs Large spoon (rice)	Fish fork and knife	Guéridon (accumulation plate)
Large warm plate Pair of tongs	Fish fork and knife Hand wipes (crayfish)	Guéridon (accumulation plate)
Large warm plate Pair of tongs	Fish fork and knife	Guéridon (accumulation plate)

SERVICE EQUIPMENT	EQUIPMENT USED TO SERVE	RECOMMENDED SERVICE STYLE
Large set-up plate Pair of tongs	Fish fork and knife (hand wipes optional)	English
Large set-up plate Warm deep plate Ladle Large fork	Fish fork Knife (optional) Dessert spoon Hand wipes	Guéridon (table stove)
Large set-up plate Small individual muscle dish	Fish fork and knife	Plate service

DISH	DISH DESCRIPTION WHEN SERVING
SEAFOOD PILAU	• Pilau rice presented in turban on an American-style sauce, garnished with prawns, muscles, scallops, langoustine tails and crayfish.

BUTCHER MEAT

DISH	DISH DESCRIPTION WHEN SERVING
POT-AU-FEU	• Beef (steak, topside, shoulder, brisket rib, hock bone and marrowbone) cooked in water with an aromatic garnish, served with vegetables (carrots, turnips, leeks, potatoes, celery). • Horseradish or ravigote sauce, mustard, salt crystals, gherkins.
TRADITIONAL BLANQUETTE DE VEAU CREOLE RICE	• Pieces of veal shoulder poached in a white sauce or in water with an aromatic garnish. • Sauce made from the reduced juices combined with cream and egg yolks. • Garnished with mushrooms and little onions. • Boiled rice.
RACK OF LAMB WITH EARLY VEGETABLES	• Full rack of lamb cooked in the oven and served with vegetables (carrots, turnips, peas, green beans, hash browns) • Gravy served separately.
RACK OF LAMB WITH PARSLEY MIXED VEGETABLES	• Full rack of lamb roasted in the oven and coated in parsley (butter, garlic, parsley, bread crumbs) • Same garnish as the early vegetables but with added artichoke and cauliflower. • Gravy served separately.
ROASTED LEG OF LAMB POTATO GRATIN	• Roasted English lamb saddle served with its gravy • Potatoes sliced into thin circles and cooked in butter in cake form
ROASTED LAMB SADDLE POMMES ANNA	• Roasted English lamb saddle served with its gravy. • Potatoes sliced into thin rounds and cooked in butter in cake form.
ROASTED SIRLOIN MIXED VEGETABLES	• Roasted beef sirloin served with its gravy. • Vegetables cut into sticks, boiled and shocked in ice, and sweated in butter.
MARÉCHALE LAMB CHOPS	• Breaded lamb chops fried in butter. • Asparagus tips or peas and truffle slices.
LITTLE STROGONOF FILLETS PILAU RICE	• Sautéed diced beef fillet. • Cream sauce. • Rice cooked in the oven with onions, butter and a bouquet garni
PEPPER STEAK POTATOES SAUTÉED RAW	• Thick sirloin or rump steak covered in a crushed pepper sauce, sautéed in cognac flambéed butter. • Sauce made from white wine, stock, cream and butter. • Potato circles pan-fried in oil and finished with butter.
BERCY SAUTÉD STEAK PAN-FRIED POTATOES	• Sautéed sirloin steak. • Sauce made from shallots, white wine, a thick brown veal stock, butter and parsley. • Potato circles cooked with their skin and sautéed in butter.
CHÂTELAINE SAUTÉED TENDERLOIN ROUND	• Beef tenderloin round sautéed in butter and served on a crouton. • Sauce made from white wine, thick brown veal stock and butter. • Served with sweated artichoke hearts and pommes noisettes.
MASCOTTE SAUTÉED TENDERLOIN ROUND	• Same recipe as the châtelaine tenderloin round served instead with artichoke hearts, pommes cocottes, steamed tomatoes and truffle slices.

SERVICE EQUIPMENT	EQUIPMENT USED TO SERVE	RECOMMENDED SERVICE STYLE
Large warm plate Pair of tongs	Large knife Large fork (or fish cutlery)	Guéridon (accumulation plate)

SERVICE EQUIPMENT	EQUIPMENT USED TO SERVE	RECOMMENDED SERVICE STYLE
Large warm plate Pair of tongs Enough dessert spoons for the accompaniments (sometimes served in a deep plate)	Large knife Large fork	Guéridon (table stove)
Large warm plate Pair of tongs Large spoon (rice)	Large knife Large fork	Guéridon (accumulation plate)
Large warm plate 2 Pair of tongs (for the vegetables) Dessert spoon (sauce boat)	Large knife Large fork Mustard	Guéridon (table stove) Gravy: English
Large warm plate 2 Pair of tongs Dessert spoon (sauce boat)	Large knife Large fork Mustard	Guéridon (table stove) Gravy: English
Large warm plate 2 Pair of tongs Dessert spoon (sauce boat)	Large knife Large fork Mustard	Guéridon (table stove) Gravy: English
Large warm plate 2 Pair of tongs	Large knife Large fork.	Guéridon (accumulation plate)
Large warm plate 2 Pair of tongs Dessert spoon (sauce boat)	Large knife Large fork Mustard	Guéridon (table stove) Gravy: English
Large warm plate 2 Pair of tongs Dessert spoon (sauce boat)	Large knife Large fork Mustard	Guéridon (table stove) Gravy: English
Large warm plate Pair of tongs	Large knife Large fork	Guéridon (accumulation plate)
Large warm plate Pair of tongs Large spoon (rice)	Large knife Large fork	Guéridon (table stove)
Large warm plate 2 pairs of Pair of tongs	Large knife Large fork	Guéridon (table stove)
Large warm plate Pair of tongs	Large knife Large fork	Guéridon (accumulation plate)
Large warm plate Pair of tongs	Large knife Large fork	Guéridon (accumulation plate)

DISH	DISH DESCRIPTION WHEN SERVING
VEAL ESCALOPE OR RIBS IN CREAM BOILED PEAS	• Veal escalope or ribs sautéed and served with button mushrooms. • Port and cream sauce. • Boiled peas sweated in butter.
VIENNESE VEAL ESCALOPE POTATOES SAUTÉED RAW	• Veal escalope (thin topside, silverside or knuckle slice) breaded and sautéed. • Garnished with lemon, olives, anchovies, capers, chopped egg yolks and whites and parsley. • Potato circles pan-fried in oil and finished with butter.
MILANESE VEAL ESCALOPE	• Veal escalope (thin topside, silverside or knuckle slice) breaded with parmesan and sautéed. • Sauce made from a tomato and Madeira wine base, garnished with mushrooms, ham, pickled beef tongue and truffle. • Spaghetti with Milanese sauce, cooked tomatoes and parmesan or gruyère.
DUROC VEAL MEDALLIONS POMMES NOISETTES	• Veal medallion (thick fillet or topside slice) sautéed in butter. • Sauce made from Cognac, white wine, shallots, mushrooms, thick brown veal stock, tomatoes and fine herbs. • Little potatoes browned in oil and finished with butter.
CHARCUTIÈRE PORK RIBS POTATO PURÉE	• Sautéed pork ribs. • Sauce made from onions, white wine, thick brown veal stock, mustard and a gherkin julienne.
LAMB CHOPS VERT-PRÉ	• Grilled lamb chops. • Served with herb butter (softened butter with parsley and lemon), watercress and straw potatoes.
MIXED GRILL	• Grilled meat selection (lamb chops, beef fillet, veal medallions, chipolatas, lamb kidneys, bacon). • Accompanied by straw potatoes, grilled mushrooms and tomatoes. • Served with herb butter (softened butter with lemon and parsley).
GRILLED BEEF RIBS OR ENTRECOTE STEAKS SAUCE BORDELAISE POTATO CROQUETTES	• Grilled beef cut (usually for 2 to 3 people) • Reduced sauce made from red wine and spices, enriched with little bone marrow dice. • Little potato purée rolls bound by egg yolk, breaded and fried.
GRILLED STEAK BÉARNAISE SAUCE POMMES PONT-NEUF	• Grilled beef cut (sirloin). • Emulsion sauce made from shallots, tarragon, chervil, pepper, egg yolks and butter. • Potatoes cut into thick sticks and deep-fried.
GRILLED RIB STEAK CHORON SAUCE POMMES PONT-NEUF	• Grilled rib steak. • Tomato Béarnaise sauce. • Potatoes cut into thick sticks and deep-fried.
HAM STEAK SPINACH LEAVES WITH BROWN BUTTER	• Grilled thick York ham slice. • Served with spinach in butter.
CHOISY RACK OF VEAL	• Full rack of lamb cooked in the oven. • Garnished with braised lettuce and egg-shaped browned potatoes. • Thick and well-seasoned gravy served separately.
BOURGEOISE BRAISED BEEF AIGUILLETTE	• Braised rump steak aiguillette (white wine, cognac, onions, carrots, tomatoes). • Garnished with diced veal trotter, tourné carrots, little lardons and glazed onions.
ZINGARA VEAL GRENADIN POMMES COCOTTES	• Little cut of veal braised in a tomato and Madeira wine sauce, garnished with a mushroom juilienne, pickled beef tongue, ham and truffle. • Olive-shaped tourné browned potatoes.

SERVICE EQUIPMENT	EQUIPMENT USED TO SERVE	RECOMMENDED SERVICE STYLE
Large warm plate Pair of tongs Large spoon (peas)	Large knife Large fork	Guéridon (accumulation plate)
Large warm plate 2 pairs of Pair of tongs	Large knife Large fork	Guéridon (accumulation plate)
Large warm plate 2 pairs of Pair of tongs Dessert spoon (sauces)	Large knife Large fork Large spoon(spaghetti)	Guéridon (table stove)
Large warm plate Pair of tongs Large spoon (potatoes)	Large knife Large fork	Guéridon (accumulation plate)
Large warm plate Pair of tongs Large spoon (potatoes)	Large knife Large fork	Guéridon (accumulation plate)
Large warm plate 2 Pair of tongs 2 dessert spoons (herb butter in a sauce boat)	Large knife Large fork	Guéridon (accumulation plate) Herb butter: Guéridon
Large warm plate	Large knife Large fork Mustard	Plate service
Large warm plate Pair of tongs Dessert spoon (sauce)	Large knife Large fork	Guéridon (accumulation plate) Sauce: English style
Large warm plate Pair of tongs Dessert spoon (sauce)	Large knife Large fork	Guéridon (accumulation plate) Sauce: English style
Large warm plate Pair of tongs Dessert spoon (sauce)	Large knife Large fork	Guéridon (accumulation plate) Sauce: English style
Large warm plate 2 pairs of Pair of tongs	Large knife Large fork Mustard	English
Large warm plate Pair of tongs Dessert spoon (sauce)	Large knife Large fork Mustard	Guéridon (table stove) Sauce: English style
Large warm plate Pair of tongs	Large knife Large fork	Guéridon (table stove)
Large warm plate Pair of tongs Large spoon (potatoes)	Large knife Large fork	Guéridon (accumulation plate)

DISH	DISH DESCRIPTION WHEN SERVING	
LAMB CURRY MADRAS RICE	• Lamb (shoulder) stew with curry, coconut milk, banana, pineapple, apple and tomato. • Rice cooked in the oven with butter, onions, grated coconut and Corinth raisins, served with almond flakes.	
BEEF BOURGUIGNON ESTOUFFADE BUTTER NOODLES	• Beef stew (topside or chuck) in red wine, garnished with lardons, button mushrooms and little onions.	
PROVENÇALE BEEF ESTOUFFADE BUTTER NOODLES	• Beef stew (topside or chuck) in white wine and tomato, garnished with green olives.	
GOULASH STEAMED POTATOES	• Tomato beef stew with onions and paprika. • Steamed potatoes	
NAVARIN WITH POTATOES	• Lamb or mutton (shoulder, breast, neck) tomato stew, garnished with little glazed onions and tourné egg-shaped potatoes.	
NAVARIN PRINTANIÈRE	• Lamb or mutton (shoulder, breast, neck) tomato stew, garnished with little onions, carrots, turnips, potatoes, peas and green beans.	
MILANESE OSSO BUCCO	• Braised veal shank roll, coated in a brown sauce made from white wine, tomatoes, orange zest and lemon. • Served with spaghetti with parmesan, cooked tomatoes and Milanese garnish in a sauce boat (see Milanese veal escalope).	
PIEDMONTESE BUCCO OSSO	• Same recipe as for the Milanese osso bucco but with a Piedmontese garnish: creamed pilau rice, parmesan and diced ham.	
MARENGO VEAL STEAMED POTATOES	• Veal (shoulder) tomato stew, garnished with little onions, mushrooms and fried croutons. • Steamed potatoes	

OFFAL

SAUTÉED VEAL LIVER ENGLISH	• Reasonably thin slice of veal, lightly floured and covered in a slice of smoked pork belly. • Steamed potatoes	
SAUTÉED VEAL KIDNEYS WITH MUSHROOMS AND MADEIRA WINE LYONNAISE POTATOES	• Thin kidney slices sautéed with mushrooms, served with Madeira sauce. • Potato circles sautéed in cooked onions.	
BRAISED VEAL SWEETBREADS COUNTRY PEAS	• Veal sweetbreads pricked with lard and braised in a spiced Madeira wine and port stock. • Sweated peas with lettuce, little onions, carrots and turnips.	

POULTRY

POACHED POULARDE SUPREME SAUCE PILAU RICE	• Poached poularde in a spiced stock, coated in a sauce made from the reduced cooking juices and cream. • Rice cooked in the oven with onions, butter and a bouquet garni	
ROAST CHICKEN MATCHSTICK POTATOES	• Oven-roasted chicken served with its gravy. • Potatoes cut into little sticks and deep-fried.	
ROASTED GUINEA FOWL ON A CANAPÉ POTATO WAFFLES	• Oven-roasted guinea fowl served on a bread crouton and sweated, with a poultry liver, shallot, lard and cognac stuffing. • Gravy served separately. • Deep fried thin potato waffle circles.	

SERVICE EQUIPMENT	EQUIPMENT USED TO SERVE	RECOMMENDED SERVICE STYLE
Large warm plate Pair of tongs Large spoon (rice)	Large knife Large fork	Guéridon (table stove)
Large warm plate 2 pairs of Pair of tongs	Large knife Large fork	Guéridon (table stove)
Large warm plate 2 pairs of Pair of tongs	Large knife Large fork	Guéridon (table stove)
Large warm plate Pair of tongs Large spoon (potatoes)	Large knife Large fork	Guéridon (table stove)
Large warm plate Pair of tongs	Large knife Large fork	Guéridon (table stove)
Large warm plate Pair of tongs	Large knife Large fork	Guéridon (table stove)
Large warm plate 2 pairs of Pair of tongs Dessert spoon (sauces)	Large knife Large fork Large spoon	Guéridon (table stove)
Large warm plate Large spoon (rice) Dessert spoon (parmesan)	Large knife Large fork	Guéridon (table stove)
Large warm plate Pair of tongs Large spoon (potatoes)	Large knife Large fork	Guéridon (table stove)

SERVICE EQUIPMENT	EQUIPMENT USED TO SERVE	RECOMMENDED SERVICE STYLE
Large warm plate Pair of tongs Large spoon (potatoes)	Large knife Large fork	Guéridon (accumulation plate)
Large warm plate 2 pairs of Pair of tongs	Large knife Large fork	Guéridon (table stove)
Large warm plate Pair of tongs	Large knife Large fork	Guéridon (table stove)

SERVICE EQUIPMENT	EQUIPMENT USED TO SERVE	RECOMMENDED SERVICE STYLE
Large warm plate Pair of tongs Large spoon (rice) Dessert spoon (sauce)	Large knife Large fork	Guéridon (table stove)
Large warm plate 2 Pair of tongs Dessert spoon (gravy)	Large knife Large fork	Guéridon (table stove) Gravy: English
Large warm plate 2 Pair of tongs Dessert spoon (gravy)	Large knife Large fork	Guéridon (table stove)

DISH	DISH DESCRIPTION WHEN SERVING
HUNTER'S CHICKEN POMMES NOISETTES	• The chicken is quartered then stewed. • Sauce made from cognac, white wine, shallots, mushrooms, thick brown veal stock and fine herbs. • Little potato circles browned in oil and finished with butter.
AMERICAN-STYLE GRILLED CHICKEN DEVIL'S SAUCE	• Whole chicken split down the back and flattened, grilled, coated in mustard and breaded, garnished with tomatoes, bacon, grilled button mushrooms, watercress and straw potatoes. • Sauce made from shallots, pepper, white wine vinegar, thick brown tomato veal stock and fine herbs.
PAN-FRIED DUCKLING WITH TURNIPS	• Duckling cooked in the oven with a white and Madeira wine sauce. • Garnished with little onions and turnips.
ORANGE DUCKLING POTATO WAFFLES	• Duckling cooked in the over with an orange and "orange liqueur" sauce. • Garnished with orange quarters. • Deep fried thin potato waffle circles.
PAN-FRIED DUCKLING WITH OLIVES	• Duckling cooked in the oven with a white and Madeira wine sauce. • Garnished with pitted green olives.
PAN-FRIED DUCKLING WITH PEAS	• Duckling cooked in the oven with a white and Madeira wine sauce. • Garnished with peas, lettuce, onions, carrots and turnips.
POULET COCOTTE GRAND-MÈRE	• Oven-cooked chicken. • Garnished with little onions, button mushrooms, lardons and little potatoes.
TRADITIONAL POULTRY FRICASSÉE PILAU RICE	• Poultry cuts cooked in a poultry and cream sauce. • Garnished with little onions and mushrooms. • Rice cooked in the oven with onions, butter and a bouquet garni
YOUNG RABBIT WITH MUSHROOMS POTATO FONDANTS	• Young rabbit cuts sautéed in butter and cooked in a shallot, white wine, brown tomato stock and mushroom sauce. • Large tourné potatoes cooked in the oven in butter and consommé.

DESSERTS

LAYERED BAVAROIS	• Dessert made from custard and whipped cream, set with gelatine and flavoured with vanilla, coffee and chocolate.
STRAWBERRY CHARLOTTE	• Dessert made from strawberry purée and whipped cream set with gelatine and surrounded by sponge fingers. • Served with a strawberry coulis (strawberry purée, sugar and lemon juice).
UPSIDE-DOWN CRÈME CARAMEL	• Flan made from milk, eggs and sugar on a caramel base.
FLAN POTS (VANILLA, COFFEE, CHOCOLATE)	• Flan made from milk, egg yolks and sugar, flavoured with vanilla, coffee or chocolate and served in a pot.
FRUITS CONDÉ	• Rice pudding with egg yolks, topped with apricot jam and fruit poached in syrup, garnished with candied cherries and angelica. • Served with a kirsch and apricot sauce.
CHOCOLATE MOUSSE (IN COUPES)	• Mousse made from chocolate, butter, egg yolks and whisked whites (whisked cream made also be added).
FLOATING ISLAND	• Normal meringue (whisked egg white) shaped as an egg and poached in milk. • Served with custard (milk, egg yolks, sugar and vanilla).

SERVICE EQUIPMENT	EQUIPMENT USED TO SERVE	RECOMMENDED SERVICE STYLE
Large warm plate Pair of tongs Large spoon (potatoes)	Large knife Large fork	Guéridon (table stove)
Large warm plate Pair of tongs Dessert spoon (sauce)	Large knife Large fork	Guéridon (accumulation plate) Sauce: English style
Large warm plate Pair of tongs Dessert spoon (sauce)	Large knife Large fork	Guéridon (accumulation plate) Sauce: English style
Large warm plate 2 Pair of tongs Dessert spoon (sauce)	Large knife Large fork	Guéridon (accumulation plate) Sauce: English style
Large warm plate Pair of tongs Dessert spoon (sauce)	Large knife Large fork	Guéridon (accumulation plate) Sauce: English style
Large warm plate Pair of tongs Dessert spoon (sauce)	Large knife Large fork	Guéridon (table stove) Sauce: English style
Large warm plate Pair of tongs Dessert spoon (sauce)	Large knife Large fork	Guéridon (table stove) Sauce: English style
Large warm plate Pair of tongs Large spoon (rice)	Large knife Large fork	Guéridon (accumulation plate)
Large warm plate Pair of tongs Large spoon (potatoes)	Large knife Large fork	Guéridon (table stove)

Dessert plate Pair of tongs	Dessert spoon and fork	Guéridon
Dessert plate Pair of tongs Dessert spoon (sauce)	Dessert spoon and fork	Guéridon Sauce: English style
Dessert plate Pair of tongs	Dessert spoon and fork	Guéridon
Dessert plate Pair of tongs (or two forks)	Dessert spoon	English
Dessert plate (cold or warm) Pair of tongs Dessert spoon	Dessert spoon and fork	Guéridon May be served cold or warm
Dessert plate Pair of tongs (or two forks)	Dessert spoon	English
Dessert plate Small deep plate (or small bowl) Ladle Large fork	Dessert spoon and fork	Guéridon

DISH	DISH DESCRIPTION WHEN SERVING
DIPLOMAT PUDDING	• Dessert made from sponge fingers, milk, eggs, sugar and candied fruit soaked in kirsch. • Served with custard.
RIZ À L'IMPÉRATRICE RED FRUIT COULIS	• Rice pudding added to custard set with gelatine, whipped cream and candied fruit soaked in kirsch. • Strawberry and raspberry coulis (fruit, lemon juice, sugar).
APPLE DOUGHNUTS	• Slices of apple soaked in lemon, cinnamon and calvados, coated in batter and cooked. • Served with an apricot and calvados sauce.
APPLE CHARLOTTE	• Dessert made from apple slices sautéed in butter, with cinnamon and flambéed in calvados then placed and cooked in a mould layered with white bread slices. • Served with an apricot and calvados sauce.
SUGAR CRÊPES	• Thin pancakes made from milk, egg, flour and caster sugar, cooked in a pan and dusted with icing or caster sugar.
FILLED CRÊPES	• Crêpes filled with crème pâtissière (made from milk, egg yolk, vanilla, flour and caster sugar) and candied fruit.
LIQUEUR SOUFFLÉS	• Batter made from crème pâtissière, whisked egg whites and sponge fingers soaked in liqueur.
WHIPPED CREAM CHOUX	• Little choux buns filled with whipped cream (whisked cream and icing sugar).
CHOCOLATE AND COFFEE CREAM CHOUX AND ÉCLAIRS	• Little round or finger-shaped choux buns filled with crème pâtissière flavoured with liqueur and coffee or chocolate.
CUSTARD GÉNOISE	• Kind of sponge served with crème anglaise (made from milk, egg yolks and vanilla caster sugar).
MOKA	• Génoise soaked in syrup, filled and covered in a coffee buttercream and decorated with chopped or flaked almonds.
MILLE-FEUILLES	• Pastry made from flaked pastry layered with crème pâtissière flavoured with liqueur.
PITHIVIERS	• Pastry made from flaked pastry filled with an almond cream.
WHIPPED CREAM SAVARIN	• Cake made from a yeast cake batter in a crown shape soaked in rum and garnished with whipped cream (whisked cream with sugar and vanilla).
ALSACIAN TART	• Shortcrust pastry base topped with apple quarters and a flan cream.
FRUIT PUFF PIE	• Puff pie base topped with crème pâtissière and fruit in syrup, coated with jam.
APPLE TART	• Shortcrust pastry topped with apple compote and thin apple slices, coated in apricot jam.

SERVICE EQUIPMENT	EQUIPMENT USED TO SERVE	RECOMMENDED SERVICE STYLE
Dessert plate Pair of tongs Dessert spoon (sauce)	Dessert spoon and fork	Guéridon Sauce: English style
Dessert plate Pair of tongs Dessert spoon (sauce)	Dessert spoon and fork	Guéridon Sauce: English style
Dessert plate Pair of tongs Dessert spoon (sauce)	Dessert spoon and fork	Guéridon Sauce: English style
Dessert plate Pair of tongs Dessert spoon (sauce)	Dessert spoon and fork	Guéridon Sauce: English style
Warm dessert plate Pair of tongs	Dessert knife (or spoon) and fork Sugar shaker	English
Warm dessert plate Pair of tongs	Dessert spoon or knife and fork Sugar shaker	English
Dessert plate Pair of tongs	Dessert knife and fork	English
Dessert plate Pair of tongs	Dessert knife and fork	English
Dessert plate Pair of tongs	Dessert knife and fork	English
Dessert plate Pair of tongs Dessert knife (cutting) Dessert spoon (sauce)	Dessert spoon and fork	Guéridon Sauce: English style
Dessert plate Pair of tongs Dessert knife (cutting)	Dessert spoon and fork	Guéridon
Dessert plate Pair of tongs Dessert knife (cutting)	Dessert knife and fork	Guéridon
Dessert plate Pair of tongs Dessert knife (cutting)	Dessert knife and fork	Guéridon
Dessert plate Pair of tongs	Dessert spoon and fork	Guéridon
Dessert plate (hot or cold) Pair of tongs Dessert knife (cutting)	Dessert knife and fork	Guéridon
Dessert plate (hot or cold) Pair of tongs Dessert knife (cutting)	Dessert knife and fork	Guéridon
Dessert plate (hot or cold) Pair of tongs Dessert knife (cutting)	Dessert knife and fork	Guéridon

DISH	DISH DESCRIPTION WHEN SERVING
FRUIT MELBA (IN A COUPE)	• Poached fruit (peaches or pears) on vanilla ice cream, coated in raspberry coulis (raspberry, lemon and icing sugar coulis).
PEARS BELLE HÉLÈNE	• Syrup poached pears on vanilla ice cream, coated in chocolate sauce.
FRUIT ICE CREAM OR SORBET (IN A COUPE)	• Made from crème anglaise or fruit syrup and pulp.
FRUIT SALAD (IN A SALAD BOWL)	• Selection of fresh fruit cut, drizzled in lemon and flavoured with alcohol (optional).

SPECIAL DISHES

SEAFOOD PLATTER	• Oysters, muscles, periwinkles, clams, crayfish, sea urchins, crab...
OYSTERS	• Fine de Claire, Belon or another variety.
CAVIAR	• Different quality sturgeon eggs (ossetra, sevruga, beluga...).
FOIE GRAS	• Force-fed goose or duck liver often cooked and served in its terrine.
SMOKED SALMON	• Half smoked salmon presented on a platter
SNAILS	• Cooked in their shells in the oven with garlic and parsley butter.
BOILED EGGS	• Eggs boiled for around 3 minutes.
FLORIDA COCKTAIL	• Mix of grapefruit and orange supremes.
GRAPEFRUIT HALF	• Grapefruit cut into two equal halves, with ½ quarters pre-cut.
KIRSCH PINEAPPLE	• Fresh pineapple cut into slices and flavoured with kirsch.
TRADITIONAL FLAMBÉED FRUIT	• Fruit cooked in butter or caramel and fruit juice, flavoured with a liqueur and flambéed with alcohol (of choice) on vanilla ice cream.

SERVICE EQUIPMENT	EQUIPMENT USED TO SERVE	RECOMMENDED SERVICE STYLE
Dessert plate Coupe Platter Pair of tongs	Dessert spoon and fork	Plate service (or platter)
Dessert plate Coupe Platter Pair of tongs	Dessert spoon and fork	Plate service (or platter)
Dessert plate Coupe Platter Pair of tongs	Dessert spoon and fork	Plate service (or platter)
Dessert plate Pair of tongs	Dessert spoon and fork	Guéridon

Stand and platter	Oyster fork Pick Pair of tongs Curette	Platter on the table Hand wipes ½ lemon Butter Rye bread Shallot vinegar "Worcestershire sauce and ketchup"
Stand and platter or deep plate on a large plate (crushed ice) or a pitted oyster plate.	Oyster fork	Platter on the table or plate Hand wipes ½ lemon Butter Rye bread Shallot vinegar "Worcestershire sauce and ketchup"
Presented in the original box on crushed ice Teaspoon Dessert plate	Teaspoon Dessert knife and fork	Guéridon Butter White bread toast Lemon "Moscovite" garnish (chopped shallots and onions, sieved boiled eggs, blinis).
Dessert plate 2 large knives Pot of hot water Napkin	Dessert knife and fork	Guéridon White bread toast Butter
Large plate Slicing cutlery	Large knife Large fork	Guéridon (buffet) White bread toast Butter Lemons
Large plate Pitted snail plate	Snail Pair of tongs Snail fork	Plate service
Usually presented in an eggcup on a dessert plate.	Dessert knife Teaspoon	Plate service White bread toast Butter
Presented on a dessert plate or in a coupe.	Dessert spoon and fork	Plate service Sugar shaker
Presented on a dessert plate or in a coupe on crushed ice.	Dessert spoon	Plate service Hand wipes Sugar shaker
Dessert plate Pair of tongs	Dessert spoon and fork	Guéridon Kirsch: English style Sugar shaker
Dessert plate Ice cream coupe - Platter	Dessert spoon and fork	Guéridon

MY NOTES

MY NOTES

Printer: Toppan
10 9 8 7 6 5 4 3 2

© **Editions BPI**

1, bd des Bouvets
92000 Nanterre

www.editions-bpi.fr